Dr. Ashby does not try to "compare" the separate religions with each other, for that, he feels, is not constructive and has been done too often in the past. His aim is to acquaint the reader with a general knowledge of certain aspects of the religions today and with central and fundamental beliefs which give the religions the content and structure they have. He emphasizes the points at which they meet both in conflict and in agreement.

Today attention is focussed on the East more than at any other time in world history and intelligent people have an obligation to try to understand the traditions and ideas which influence so markedly the thoughts and actions of the teeming millions who live in that part of the world.

This book, while it will have the approval of scholars, is addressed primarily to laymen whose knowledge of the leading religions is at best elementary.

ABOUT THE AUTHOR

Since 1950, Dr. Philip H. Ashby has been a member of the faculty of Princeton University. His field is the History of Religions and he received his Ph.D. from the University of Chicago. He has been also a Visiting Lecturer at Drew Theological Seminary and at Perkins School of Theology, Southern Methodist University. During the war he saw two years of active duty in the Navy in the South and Central Pacific areas. Just recently he was the recipient of a scholarship to study in India and Ceylon as well as at Oxford University.

The Conflict of Religions

The Conflict of Religions

THE Conflict

OF Religions

Philip H. Ashby

CHARLES SCRIBNER'S SONS
NEW YORK
1955

THE Conflict

OF Religions

Philip H. Ashby

CHARLES SCRIBNER'S SONS

NEW YORK

1955

T O

My Father and Mother

in love and gratitude

PREFACE

Much of the current thought and literature of today is concerned with the terrifying problems which now confront man and his society. Speakers and writers on any serious aspect of life and thought frequently are embarrased by the necessity of introducing their discussions with the usual portrayal of the serious nature of the contemporary human situation—a scene which is already only too well known to present-day thinking men and women. This is true even when it is the hope of the speaker or writer to strike an optimistic note in the midst of the despair which is engulfing so many of his audience. Man cannot think in realistic terms concerning himself or his world, nor can he construct appropriate plans of action, unless he is adequately aware of the environment which surrounds him. He cannot afford to ignore the unpleasant, perhaps disastrous, future which may await him; nor can he be so overcome by a consciousness of it that he fails to see the signs for hope which bring rays of light into the gloom of his despair.

These pages are written with the conviction that man has at his disposal a powerful and as yet relatively untried resource whereby he can meet the troubles of this age with confidence. It is not an easy conviction which ignores the struggles which face man even if he does use the resource which is available; nor is it based on a naïve assumption that the problems of man arise from causes which will easily disappear once man approaches them with a determination to resolve them. And, most important of all, it is a conviction

which is not oblivious to the fact that the ultimate source of
the problems which plague man, is man himself.

This resource is the combined witness of the major religions
of the world. It is not at all unusual for someone to point to
religion as the hope of man in this or any age. The religions
themselves have been doing it throughout the centuries, and
discerning men and women of all levels of life have been, and
are, convinced of the value of religion for man. However,
attempts to approach the possibility of a combined witness of
the religions have been extremely limited. They have usually
been confined to a few scholars who have been intrigued by
the possibility of a synthesis of philosophical and theological
thought, or to idealists whose enthusiasm prevents them from
recognizing the real difficulties involved. Few, if any, discussions of the subject have attempted to direct themselves
to the intelligent layman whose knowledge of the leading
religions is, at best, elementary. And yet it is the thinking
layman—the man or woman who is engaged in the many and
varied pursuits which constitute contemporary world society
—who must support such a witness.

This book, therefore, is not written for the scholar, though
one hopes that it will have his approval. It attempts to present an understanding of the present conflict in which the
leading religions find themselves, though it is aware that the
scholar will all too often deplore the broad generalizations
which the author finds himself forced to make (and to which
he wishes he could attach detailed explanatory footnotes).
Further, as one who is grateful that *Comparative* Religions
has been replaced by the History of Religions, the author
hastens to add that it is his hope that the method he has used
to present his subject will not be considered as an attempt
to hold the religions up for "comparison" in the evaluative
sense. Rather, the endeavor is made to acquaint the reader
with a general knowledge of certain aspects of the religions
today, and with central and fundamental beliefs which give
the religions the content and structure they have. If any
should desire to "compare" the separate religions with each

other, it is hoped they are wise enough to seek the necessary knowledge and empathy from other sources.

There will be some who will wonder why the religions which are considered have been chosen, while others were not. The criterion has been simply on the basis of discussing those religions which now consider themselves to be universal (though even here there is room for debate), and the present appeal and strength of the religions of the world. Readers who are acquainted with the so-called Great Religions of the World will be aware that those religions which are not discussed here also have much to contribute to the general theme which is suggested in the following pages.

The suggested readings are intended merely as suggestions to those who are unacquainted with the subject in general, and who may desire to read further. As in the writing of the book itself, they are selected with the general reader in mind. Any who may desire to pursue the matter at a more detailed and technical level are referred to the many available works dealing with the various aspects of the contemporary world religions.

My indebtedness to the many scholars who have devoted their energies to coming to an understanding of the religions of the world will be obvious to those readers who are acquainted with the growing interest in the study of the History of Religions during the past century. Their number is so large that I am forced to refrain from mentioning them by name. However, I should be remiss in my duty and in my desire if I did not mention Professor Joachim Wach. Those of us who have the good fortune to be his students are conscious of his contribution to our thinking in all that we say or write. His profound scholarship may cause him to be critical of our feeble attempts to explore the academic discipline he knows so well, and our enthusiasm may take us into paths where he in his wisdom would not go, yet his continued interest in his students wherever they may be teaching or studying is a source of stimulation in all we do. The good teacher is seldom forgotten by his students; the dedicated

Christian scholar who shares his insights with gracious humility continues to inform and inspire when the formal days of instruction are only a pleasant memory.

To Princeton University, and especially to Professor George F. Thomas of the Department of Religion, I wish to express my appreciation for the opportunity to spend a year travelling and studying in India, Ceylon, and England. The chapters which follow are, I trust, but the first fruits of the freedom which they extended to me from the usual academic responsibilities for the period of a year.

Finally, how does one express gratitude to those who have to tolerate him while he is trying to put his thoughts on paper —the two children who are convinced that something world-shaking is being forged amid the din of the typewriter, and the wife who gives encouragement and who types the final manuscript? There are no words, there can only be the silence of deep-felt love.

PHILIP H. ASHBY

Princeton
July, 1955

CONTENTS

Contents

1. *RELIGION*

IN THE WEST

There are many who are convinced we are living in a time completely different from anything which mankind has experienced in the past. It is only when we read history carefully that we are brought to the realization that each age has had its conflicts and its tensions, its hopes and its achievements. Nevertheless, an awareness that other periods in man's history have been marked by convulsions and birth-pangs does not alter the conviction that, as with all events and epochs, the peculiar nature of what we are experiencing is different from that which has gone before.

When we are convinced that no age has faced problems of such magnitude as ours we are forgetting that the enormity of a thing is determined by the perspective from which it is viewed. The seeming simplicity of the conflicts of the past is apparent to us only because we possess the perspective of time and of reflection. For us the challenge of our age is overwhelming because the time is short and the outcome unknown. The factors converging to make up our problems are unique not so much in their own nature, as in the fashion in which they have united to confront us.

It is almost impossible to read a serious discussion of the world in which we live which does not remind us again and again that the earth and its peoples are now living in a period of transition and of new birth. How else is one to explain and to justify the conflicts and tensions which confront us on every hand? The passing of much that is old, and the constant appearance of that which is new, will not allow us to conclude otherwise. This is our dilemma and this is our challenge.

Religion occupies a central position among the elements which go to make up the dimension of contemporary human concern. It should not be necessary to demonstrate the prominent place religion holds in the life of mankind. The contention that new generations are turning less to religion and more to other sources for meaning and purpose in life, while perhaps demonstrable, does not alter the fact that religion continues to furnish to the great majority of men a conscious or unconscious view of the universe. It continues to serve as a basis for acting and being. It shall not be our purpose here to defend the claim of religion to consideration along with the other constituent parts of the modern scene. Even those who have dismissed religion from their own lives must, if they are objective at all, acknowledge the place of religion within the world and its centrality in any consideration of the situation which faces mankind.

Having insisted upon the place of religion, and having acknowledged that the mood of many is to dismiss religion as being a mere vestige of the past rather than a live and demanding option of the present, honesty requires us to concede that the state of religion around the world is not one of universal vibrant health. The condition of religion varies from locality to locality. It is determined by local as well as worldwide factors and influences. However, one is not far amiss in concluding that religion as a whole, along with the world in general, is facing problems which threaten to destroy it. It is failing to measure up to the opportunities and challenges of the time. Even the most active of today's religions must plead guilty to this. Those which are now in lethargy are too indolent to acknowledge such guilt, and this is their greatest weakness. The necessary first step to accomplishment by the religions of the world is an objective assessment of the situation and of their resources for the meeting of it.

Today the religions of the world find themselves not only confronted by world forces and movements which are in opposition to them and their purposes, they are the inheritors of a tradition of opposition to each other. Faced by enemies who would destroy them, they are also in conflict among themselves. Religion is the opponent of religion.

Such a situation is not simply the result of a tradition of the past. In the Western world the conflict between religions and within religions has furnished the subject matter for much of our history. This has been less true in the East. But the conflict between religions today is much more than the continuation of age-old misunderstandings or prejudices. It arises out of basic differences within their bodies of belief; it is fed by the zeal of partisanship and conviction of superiority which often accompanies religious adherence.

Because of this conflict between religions—which has existed in the past, exists now, and will likely continue to exist for some time in the future—it is essential that those who would work for the solution of the world's tensions discover the nature of the conflict between religions. Those who are committed to religion in one of its world forms, and who are concerned that what they conceive as the values of religion be preserved and utilized, cannot continue to ignore the religious conflict or attempts at its solution.

There are few things more difficult to assess correctly than the place of religion in the Western world. Competent authorities differ greatly in their conclusions as to the strengths and weaknesses of Christianity and Islam. Judaism because of its debatable racial nature is slightly easier to assess if it is considered to be identified with a particular national people. However, this identification is challenged by many Jews themselves. And even if the identification were allowed, just how does one determine to what degree the Jewish people of the world are faithful to the religion of Judaism? The presence of divergent religious groups within Judaism indicates that even a religion which appears at first glance to the layman to be a cohesive whole is not always the simple unity it appears to be on the surface.

The two conflicting religions of the West are primarily

Christianity and Islam. Western history for fourteen hundred years has been concerned with the open conflicts and subtle contests between these two religions. The early years of Muslim history were marked by the military successes of the Arab peoples and their converts as they swept great areas of Christendom before them. Spurred on by a religious faith and brotherhood, the growing military, cultural, and economic strength of the Near Eastern world created for itself an empire and civilization which has continued in one form or another down to the present century. Sharing much in common in religious belief and tradition, Islam and Christianity were separated nevertheless by religion, culture, and the demands of political empire. From the days of the conquering Caliphs, through the religious fervor of the Crusades, down to the modern contest of missions, these two religions have faced each other as opponents.

There have been isolated periods in Western history when the thought processes of the two contenders have achieved a certain harmony. Feeding upon common resources in their intellectual expressions, both Islam and Christianity have placed themselves in debt to each other. The student of Western philosophy and of Christian theology cannot ignore the place of certain Muslim thinkers who served as the carriers of early Greek and Eastern Mediterranean thought to the Scholastics of the Middle Ages. The interplay of thought between Christian, Muslim, and Jewish thinkers has left all three faiths enriched by the experience.

However, as important as such interconnections may be, they must always be seen as but isolated occurrences in the long history of Christian-Muslim relationships. They indicate the possibility of fruitful interchange between the religions and their thought. They do not establish the fact that such relationships will come about as the result of direct purpose. Such interchanges were the unintended but natural results of growing vitality within each of the religions. History has demonstrated that when this vitality is not present such fruitful interrelationships will not only not occur, they will be deliberately avoided. When we seek to come to an understanding of the religious situation in the Western world today we must recognize the possibility of mutual cross fertilization between Islam and Christianity while we remember that the mood of both religions has seldom, if ever, deliberately encouraged such rapport.

Religious leaders who desire that religion in the West be active in the creation of a world order which will surmount the problems of our day are directly confronted by the question as to whether they will look favorably upon co-operation between these two historic contenders. Their answer to that question during the decades which are immediately ahead may well decide the future of the world as well as the continued existence of the religions which they represent. Acknowledgment of the need of such co-operation is not, as some would claim, evidence of a lack of faithfulness to the religion of which one is a part. Rather, it is indicative of a deep desire to serve that religion well in the face of great responsibilities which demand venturesome thinking and heroic action.

1. Christianity in Conflict

The history of Christianity is a record of constant conflict. There has been conflict with the environment which surrounded Christianity, and conflict within Christianity itself. The first centuries of the Christian movement were times calling for heroic witness of the Christian message in an environment which was hostile. With the apparent victory of Christianity in the latter days of the Roman Empire it appeared that the conflict was resolved, but the resolution was one of appearance only and not of fact. Confronted with the task of establishing Christianity within the Greco-Roman world as the way of life and ground of thought, the Christian Church continued in conflict with the established mores, customs, and religions of the Mediterranean and European areas. It was only when the Church had apparently succeeded in its purpose that the conflict subsided. It was then that the way was open for the appearance of decisive conflicts within the body of the Church—conflicts which unlike their forerunners were of greater consequence because the Church had lost its vitality when it ceased in its antagonism toward the environment around it.

Thus, there appeared recognizable divisions within Christianity. These divisions came to be recognized by each other as actual, if not legitimate, to the degree that time brought into being a working relationship between at least some of the divisions themselves. Again, it would appear that the conflict had been resolved, and if not resolved, at least accepted as a continuing factor within the body of Christendom.

The development of currents of life and thought which created the modern secular life of the West, however, brought the divergent bodies of Christianity into open conflict with their environment. Where one of the groups within organized Christianity might in some fashion be aligned with a secular movement, others would declare themselves to be in opposition to that movement. Scientism, nationalism, colonialism, capitalism, industrialism, socialism—these and similar movements within Western life each presented opportunities and problems to the separate branches of the Christian religion. The well-known conflict between Christianity and science is but one example of religion confronted by a problem of great magnitude—a problem which it cannot escape without weakening itself and strengthening its opponent. And as in so many cases of like nature, Christianity's claim to having met the problem is more superficial than it is actual. A peace has been declared, but many of the religious bodies of Christendom have not yet finished their task of adjustment to those aspects of modern science which cannot be accepted or rejected easily.

A. CHRISTIANITY: THE ENCOUNTER WITH THE PRESENT

The conflict between Christianity and the spirit of our times is an antagonism which is often forgotten by the lay member of the Church. He has adapted himself successfully to a bifurcated life wherein the division and hostilities of his two realms of existence apparently are forgotten. In some instances he has adjusted the claims of one area to the demands of the other. This has been true especially in the confusion of modern Western culture or of a particular nationalism with the Christian gospel. The way of life and the values of a people or a political unit subtly but definitely have been accepted as being the incarnation of the teachings of the Christian religion.

For many outside the Church the conflict is no more apparent. Looking upon much of the belief and practice of worship in Christianity as being a vestige of the past they do not commit themselves to it. Yet, they do find that there is something within the total message of Christianity which holds meaning for them. It may be of no more consequence than that they are disturbed if they or their children are without the customary basic sacraments of the Christian faith. They are faced with an inner compulsion therefore to participate occasionally in Christian rites, and they often give lip service to the basic dogmas of Christianity in its broad form. They cannot make Christianity a central aspect of their lives, yet they cannot bring themselves to turn their backs completely upon it. They are the victims of the conflict of essential Christianity with the underlying spirit of their times, but they are unaware of their tragic situation.

Again, there are others who are outside the Church because of their consciousness of the conflict. For them the dichotomy demanded is too great. Deeply aware of their attachment to the secular ethos in which they live, their native integrity prevents them from paying lip service to Christianity. They refuse to be caught in the position of serving two masters, neither of whom can be served successfully if any consideration is given to the other. Yet even for these there is often the conviction that they are somehow in relationship with the essence of the Christian Faith. Their commitments demand that they declare their allegiance to the way of life which is demanded by the spirit of the times, but their inner yearnings, and an inexplicable certitude, convinces them that there is a relationship between themselves and the source of their being to which they are not completely untrue.

Western man in the contemporary world is forced into this embarrassing position by the essential nature of the Christian-religious faith which he inherits, and by the character of the social environment in which he must live. Despite the fact that each of these has in varying degrees shaped the other, they remain in conflict because of the divergent character of their aims and motivations. Christianity is concerned with man's life in this world but it cannot allow human society's all-consuming passion with the things of material existence to be supreme. On the other hand, society is concerned with the fulfilment of man, but it does not conceive of that fulfilment as lying outside or beyond the bounds of earthly existence.

It is against this human preoccupation with the things of this world that Christianity protests. And in its protestation the Church finds itself seemingly in direct opposition to the very welfare of mankind itself. Caught in the dilemma of wishing material well-being for man while seeking that he also be not limited to the material, Christianity has not escaped being misunderstood by its adherents as well as by its foes.

Christianity has prided itself on being a religion which views happenings in the dimension of time and space as real events—events which are of consequence to both man and God. Convinced that man does not live by bread alone, it also has the example of One who fed mankind with bread as He taught of spiritual things. It is this dual responsibility of concern with the material while emphasizing the insufficiency of it that has created for Christianity much of the dilemma which is confronting it today.

Christianity is not only in conflict with modern secularism. It is in conflict with the very concept of secularism. Christianity is an inheritor of the Semitic-Hebrew conception of all existence as being an integrated whole. There is no secular and spiritual; no two-storied world divided into the realms of time and eternity with an iron walled division between them. For Christianity no area of life can exist which is outside or beyond the range of Christian concern. There is no region where the Christian gospel is not relevant; there is no event or concern in human life which may properly be said to be of no consequence to God.

Therefore, Christianity finds itself not only in conflict with the apparent interests of its adherents in its opposition to the secular life of society, it also is brought into conflict with its own essential nature in the degree that it seeks to adjust to the secular demands of modern society. Christianity is a religion of human beings as well as a religion with a divine source. As it seeks to maintain its contact with humanity it runs the danger of succumbing to the demands of humanity. Where those demands are of such a nature that they require a softening of the claims of the Divine, in meeting the human demands Christianity may well find itself in conflict with itself. The Christian religion, like its people, finds itself to be disjointed. In fact it is because the religion has not been constant in its preaching and claims concerning the unity of existence that Western Christians themselves have lost the consciousness of that unity.

There are those within the Church who are not only ready to admit the existence of such a situation but who are seeking by every means to call Christians to the task of breaking down the barriers between the secular world of today and the Christian gospel. They are the ones who often face the accusation of being revolutionaries, even anti-Christian. They are confronted by the conviction of many within the Church that the established order of things is somehow divinely ordained. As they seek to bring all existence and human activity under the judgment of God they are met with the spirit of the times which has concluded either that there is no God, or if there is, He has a separate sphere of existence which is not concerned with what goes on in the market place of human life.

This, briefly, is the conflict of Christianity with the secular spirit which dominates our age. It is a conflict which is the result not only of the convergence of many currents which go to make up the modern world; it is a result of an abdication by Christianity of its total claim upon human existence as it has attempted to meet the demands of humanity. The encounter is inevitable as Christianity continues to become more conscious of its duty to both God and man.

B. CHRISTIANITY: THE INTERNAL TENSIONS

Christianity also finds itself in conflict with itself. Not only does tension exist between the claims of the Divine and the human, Christianity is confronted by discord within itself institutionally. The separation of Christianity into Roman Catholic, Eastern Orthodox, and Protestant; the existence of institutional forms of Church, denomination, and sect; the sometimes violent disagreements between Protestant groups; the exclusiveness of Christian groups and their suspicions of one another in matters of theology and local church policy— all of these indicate that a survey of Christianity must be extremely careful in treating it as a unity. These divisions and disagreements in conceptions of the Christian Faith theologically and organizationally cannot be minimized or glossed over in the current enthusiasm over co-operation between the various branches of organized Christianity.

The institutional conflict within Christianity reflects the tension between authority and freedom which is ever present within religion. No religion has completely escaped the problem as to what degree authority must be recognized for the sake of religious uniformity, least of all the Western religions with their Semitic inheritance. If authority is recognized as being basic to the institutional system and theological formulations of the religion, just what limitations, if any, shall be placed upon that authority? This has posed the question whether the Christian Faith shall be bound by authority to the degree that freedom of religious insight and experience shall be limited to those forms acceptable to the authority, or whether greater or complete freedom shall be allowed. Will not such freedom by its very nature serve to weaken the supremacy of the authority? And if the authority is not supreme, but is qualified, what shall serve to preserve the essential nature and form of the Faith?

Further, the situation within Christianity wherein its various components appear to be striving in opposition to each other is a manifestation of the demand for authoritarian certitude which is particularly characteristic of the West, although not completely absent in the East. This demand expresses itself in the rise of separate groups claiming to possess Absolute Truth. Clustered about a common central theme and historically dependent upon each other in a multitude of ways, these groups claim superiority over each other in their particular exposition of that theme. The fact that the past century has seen the development of greater understanding between some of these groups does not alter the serious nature of this aspect of Christianity. For at the same time that some of the more influential groups within Protestantism have come to recognize the value of each other, small but not inconsequential groups have risen to renew the separateness which the larger groups are seeking to overcome.

The most obvious conflict of organized Christianity with itself is to be found in the existence of the Roman Catholic and Protestant expressions of the Christian Faith. A close reading of history establishes that this break was not alone due to specifically religious or theological concerns. The Reformation must always be considered in the light of political, intellectual, economic, and social developments before and during the sixteenth century, as well as in the context of theological-ecclesiastical matters. The very fact of the impingement of secular concerns upon such a vital event in Christian history gives evidence of the close relationship between a religion and the ethos in which it is placed. If it desires to be dynamic in any age, a religion must recognize that the problems of that age, and its own articulation of its message, must be conceived jointly.

The continuation of the breach between these two large divisions of Christianity cannot be claimed to be due to any one specific factor. We shall have occasion later to point to some theological aspects of the continuing division. However, the Protestant rejection of papal authority, and the Roman Catholic insistence upon that authority continues to lie at the very core of the separation. From the Roman Catholic position any move toward rapprochement can only proceed on the basis of Protestant acceptance of the principle of papal supremacy at least in matters of faith and morals, if not in affairs of ecclesiastical organization. For Protestantism to accept such a demand is to retreat from what it has considered to be one of the great contributions of the Reformation to Christianity.

The growing acceptance in Protestant circles of the place of the lay Christian in the development of theological thought and the direction of the ecclesiastical institution has created a further difficulty in any attempts which might be made in the direction of joining the two contenders. Roman Catholicism has not forgotten the place of the layman in the Church. However, the conception of just what is the place of the layman is not of the same character as that possessed in the majority of Protestant circles today. In Roman Catholicism the theory of the priesthood results in the layman taking a subordinate role in both theological matters and institutional control. In Protestantism the layman is conceived as being a partner in the direction of the institution and the articulation of the gospel to the age of which the layman is a part. The fact that the layman may have abdicated from this responsibility during various periods of Protestant history has not altered the Protestant insistence upon the fundamental freedom of the Christian layman in matters of faith and in creating religious organizations of his own choosing.

While we cannot allow ourselves a detailed investigation of the continuing causes for the major division within the ranks of Christianity, it is necessary at least to point to the divergent views held by the two groups in regard to the separation of Church and State. For the Roman Catholic such a separation is a denial of the central authority and place of the Christian

Church in human life and affairs. It has only been in those areas where Catholicism has been forced to accept such a situation that she has adjusted herself to that which is demanded of her. But such acceptance has not changed the basic position of Roman Catholicism in the matter. And there are those Protestants who are becoming more and more convinced that the Roman Catholic Church has not yet accepted as final her role as one Christian group among many in those societies where such is now the situation.

The divergency of views concerning the relationship between Christianity and the secular political power is particularly important in view of the growing tendency toward centralization and uniformity in Western society. The principle of separation between church organization and political authority, while not necessarily implying a separation of religion itself from the political affairs of society, has contributed greatly to the religious and secular division of Western life. In recognizing that only by such separation could religious liberty be insured, Protestant Christianity placed upon itself the great burden of exercising Christian influence in the political affairs of society by means of religious teaching and persuasion. All too often the separation has been misunderstood as being both an abdication of concern and responsibility.

The existence of the conflict within Christianity between varying organized groups each seeking to be *the* Christian Church, while being of paramount importance in any consideration of Christianity in the world today, does not mean that these groups do not possess a conception of the unity of Christianity. Even those sectarian bodies which look upon themselves as being the chosen and true representatives of the Christian gospel are deeply conscious of the fact that all those who are followers of Christ are bounded together into a unity. Thus for them the conviction that others who follow Christ are being misled by mistaken theological beliefs or practices assumes tragic importance. They are impelled by this belief to seek by every means to bring the divergent groups of

Christianity into what they conceive to be the correct relationship to the Christian gospel.

Those groups which have ceased in the present day to place strong emphasis upon their own separate existence are especially concerned with the fact of Christianity in conflict with itself. They, in particular, are conscious of the tragedy of Christian separation. Some leaders within Protestant groups have looked to Roman Catholicism with the hope that they might establish a fellowship which would result eventually in unity. The Oxford Movement of the last century and the Anglo-Catholic movement today, both within the Anglican Church, are indicative of the hope for Christian institutional unity on the part of certain Protestant groups.

The major denominational groups within Protestantism, in conjunction with their growing awareness of the need for a united effort in presenting the Christian gospel, have been engaged in united projects which have brought them to the threshold of spiritual unity if not organic oneness. Co-operative consideration of missions, of religious education of youth, and like projects has created a consciousness of identity in the Christian task which has blossomed in the past decades into concrete attempts toward a more unified institutional form. The creation of councils of Churches on the local, national, and international level, and the accompanying ecumenical spirit, have brought new heart to those for whom Christian separateness is the denial of the basic spirit of the Christian gospel.

C. CHRISTIANITY: THE VARIETY OF THOUGHT

The conflict of Christianity with the spirit of the times, and the divisions within Christian ranks are accompanied by a conflict of thought within the Christian Faith. This conflict of thought within the body of Christianity has been the cause out of which much of the division has arisen. One cannot refrain from wondering, also, if the inability of Christianity to meet the problems of mankind does not stem in large measure from the clash in theological interpretation which has accompanied so much of Christian history both past and present.

The institutional separation between Roman Catholicism and Protestantism, to which we have referred, ultimately finds its greatest reason for being in the differences of theological thought which separate contemporary Catholicism and Protestantism. The Roman Catholic concern for papal authority arises out of a conception of the Christian Faith which differs from Protestant thought on theological grounds. Attempts to find scriptural or historical evidence supporting papal authority have little meaning to Protestants even if they were to accept the evidence as genuine. While there are those Protestant groups who do have a high sense of the Church as a divinely ordained community, yet the general tenor of sentiment within Protestantism is not one which will in any way accept that community nor its head as being beyond the range of human criticism. This stems from a deep awareness of the nature of human frailty, as well as a consciousness of the need of man for freedom from institutional limitations in his religious life. For the Protestant, divine influence in human affairs if not more limited is at least of a different character than that which the Catholic conceives to be the case in regard to the Church.

As with all religions, Christianity is continually confronted by the problem of superstition and the inclination of its members to hold to beliefs of the past which are now challenged as not being worthy nor true to the highest Christian insights. Both Protestantism and Roman Catholicism have faced, and continue to face this problem. Catholicism's deep consciousness of Christian tradition and history has made it vulnerable to the Protestant charge that it continues to be enmeshed in unworthy beliefs and practices of the past. It must be said that there are those among the Catholic clergy and laity who are aware of the seriousness of this charge, but who rightly point out that Protestantism itself is not completely free from the problem.

The division within Christianity in this regard might properly be said to be not so much a conflict between separate institutional forms of the Faith as it is a conflict between two levels of religion. These two levels are to be found in all religions, and they reflect the struggle between the intellectual and non-intellectual religious person.

Both Roman Catholicism and Protestantism exhibit and produce religious insights and practices which rise far beyond lower levels of superstition and magic, while at the same time large numbers of their membership continue to seek and find in Christianity aspects of belief and practice which are repugnant to the more educated adherents of the same religious faith.

The student of religion is faced with the necessity of distinguishing between these levels of the same religion. It makes no difference to what degree a particular religion claims to be the result of divine revelation, it must also recognize that in its forms and its content it is also the product of human desires as to what religion should be. In the case of Christianity the history of the Faith is filled with the record of successive struggles against wild flights of the human imagination concerning everything from the apocalyptic end of the world to witches.

But the battle in this regard is not over. Christianity continues to be faced by expressions of belief in its various branches which are more nearly akin to primitive forms of religion than to the modern scientific view of the world. The problem is particularly acute because the conflict between Christianity and the scientific secular temper of today is continually beclouded by the prevalent impression of many outside the Church that the lower expressions of Christianity are representative of essential Christianity.

If we seek to use the term "lower" in a non-qualitative sense and simply as a means of separating one type or classification of religious belief from another, we do not escape from the fact that in the minds of many people in the West the word "lower" is fitting to be used in a qualitative sense. A Roman

Catholic dogma or a Protestant article of faith very often appears to be only a manifestation of religious superstitions of the past. It avails little that eminent Christian thinkers are able to integrate such beliefs into their own thinking.

All of this points, again, to the conflict which is present in the realm of thought within the Christian Faith. It is not, in this instance, conflict between separate brands of theology, it is conflict between the mind which seeks intellectual justification for what it holds and the mind which is not concerned with such matters. Religion in the West is thus confronted not only by struggle between itself and its environment, but also by tension within itself between its "higher" and its "lower" forms of belief and expression.

A further instance of the conflict within the body of Christianity in regard to religious belief is to be seen in the basic spirit which differentiates various groups in their approach to theology. Again, this is perhaps best seen in the general differences between Roman Catholicism and Protestantism, but it is also evident within separate branches of Protestantism. On the one hand, there is the strong insistence that there must be uniformity of thought and acceptance of belief; on the other, there is allowance and acceptance of a wide variety of interpretation. Protestantism in its more liberal moments continues to find a place for such widely divergent groups as the Anglicans and Unitarians. However, the present tendency in Protestant theological circles toward a stricter orthodoxy has led the World Council of Churches to so formulate its basis of membership that non-Trinitarians cannot subscribe to it in good faith. At the same period in Protestant history when inter-denominational co operation and understanding are so evident in certain realms of activity, theologically the conflict continues.

When we consider what more properly may be termed theological tensions within Christianity, and especially within Protestantism, we are confronted by two general divisions of thought. The first has to do with the Christian scriptures and their nature. The second is concerned with the theological interpretation of the Christian message as it arises from the scriptures and the intellectual expressions of the Faith throughout Christian history.

There are many who are unaware that the great biblical controversy which marked the last decades of the nineteenth and first years of the twentieth century is still a matter which divides much of Protestant Christianity. Fundamentalism and Modernism in regard to belief about the Bible still exists to separate great numbers of Protestant Christians in America and Europe. The Modernist, or individual who has accepted the place of literary and historical criticism in biblical studies considers that the issue is closed, but in reality it is only closed for him because he has accepted one of the two alternatives. The energy and success of the religious groups who insist upon the Fundamentalist interpretation of the Bible is one of the inescapable facts of modern Protestant history.

The differences in belief concerning the Bible which result from a literal interpretation of the scriptures as over against a view that they are of historic fallible human manufacture has created and continues to create a conflict within Christianity which easily leads to animosity between Christians even when they are motivated by the highest type of Christian love and brotherliness.

Individuals who consider themselves to be Christian and who are earnestly seeking to be worthy of the name are confronted by the challenge of others that they are not Christians if they do not accept the biblical interpretation of the creation of the world. For great numbers of Protestants an essential part of being a Christian is the acceptance of the apocalyptic-eschatological world view which is characteristic of certain of the Old Testament and New Testament books. The Modernist who views these aspects of the Christian scriptures as being reflections of the period in which they were written, and not as essential beliefs required of a modern follower of Christ, is a stranger to the Fundamentalist for whom these beliefs are essential. The two believers are in conflict with each other to the degree that they find it difficult even to tolerate one another, let alone unite in Christian worship and service.

The dissension within Protestant Christianity concerning the theological interpretation of the gospel is in some measure a continuation of the biblical controversy. For those groups which are Fundamentalist in their thinking there is little question as to how a Christian shall interpret the Faith in this or any generation. The Bible in and of itself, so they maintain, furnishes the norm for theology. The theologian is not confronted with the task of applying all the accumulated philosophical, metaphysical, and scientific thought which mankind has achieved over the centuries of intellectual history. His task is the more confined, and therefore simpler one, of catching the spirit and the content of the Bible as a whole. Not only is the truth totally within the scriptures, but that truth is self-evident and *sui generis*.

In whatever degree he accepts the results of modern biblical studies and literary criticism, the Modernist is confronted with a far more difficult task when he turns to theological exposition of the Christian gospel. For him, all the intellectual powers of man must be applied to the content of the Christian message. The Bible and its content remain the norm of theological construction for it is the central depository of the Faith, but such a theologian differs from his Fundamentalist counterpart in that he conceives it to be his task not only to discover the spirit and content of the scriptures but to demonstrate and establish the truth and values of the gospel on extra-biblical intellectual grounds as well. In this he acknowledges himself to be a part of the whole of humanity in its search for Truth, and as a participant in the intellectual spiritual quest of mankind he refuses to allow himself to be detached completely from the methods of the secular world of which he is a part. He does not view the realm of his concern as being completely super-intellectual, nor does he consider the biblical revelation of the Divine to be totally different from other aspects of the truth of existence which must be grasped by the mind of man and expressed in human fallible categories of thought.

Within each of these general theological divisions there is also ground for further disagreement. In some cases the disagreements between individual theological thinkers, or schools of thought, are readily recognized by the participants themselves as legitimate differences of opinion and conclusion arising out of the individual nature of finite men. When certain presuppositions which are considered to be fundamental are accepted, they will allow each other latitude in their method and their conclusions. However, even here actual conflict which is of a more serious nature than accepted disagreement can and does arise. Theological circle is in opposition to theological circle, and what begins as mere debate and is indicative of vitality comes dangerously near to the establishment of new divisions within the Faith.

2. Islam in Conflict

Religion in any of its forms must be recognized as being a living organism. As such, each religion exhibits variety within its own structure which is peculiar to that structure, and which is not necessarily to be found within other bodies of religious belief. In a fashion similar to the problems which beset our times, it is not so much that the specific items within a religion are different from those to be found in other religions as it is that the manner in which those items are correlated and dependent upon each other vary from religion to religion. Most religions incorporate prayer or its counterpart as an essential aspect of their total systems, but this does not imply that the object prayed to in each religion is identical. The difference is in the nature of the variety to be found among individual human beings each possessing the same general physical and psychological make-up but who, nevertheless, are to be observed as individuals and not as identical beings.

The religious world and system which is known as Islam is a living organism of theological belief and religious practice. Because it is living it possesses individuality and is in a

state of flux and movement. In company with all religions it
defies simple classification and broad generalizations of its
thought, its social structure, and the tensions which are a part
of its contemporary existence. In the task which we have set
for ourselves—of gaining an understanding of the conflicts
within and between the leading religions of the world—we are
called upon to make broad generalizations which all too often
convey the impression that that which is being discussed can
be classified simply and understood easily. While this may
be unavoidable in a discussion of such limited scope as ours,
both the writer and the reader must be reminded of the errone-
ous impression that will likely result unless it is clear that
generalizations are being made. And, since with Islam we
step outside the religious ethos which is peculiarly our own,
it is at this point that we must caution ourselves against the
dangers which beset us.

As a religion which arose at a time and a place where two
of the other great living religions of today were influential,
Judaism and Christianity, Islam in many respects may be
termed a daughter religion of Judaism and a sister religion of
Christianity. Islam has gathered within itself aspects of the
early tribal religions of the Arabian desert, of Zoroastrianism,
of Judaism, and of Christianity. However, this dependence
upon previously existing religions does not mean that Islam
does not possess within itself a uniqueness which rises above
its component parts. Just as Christianity can be understood
adequately only in relationship to its Jewish heritage and the
Hellenic influence which shaped its early history, so, too, it is
necessary to discern clearly the various wellsprings out of
which much of Islam flows.

The pre-Islamic animism of Arabia in conjunction with
the popular religious imagery of Zoroastrianism bequeathed
to Islam a substratum of superstition and imagery which
throughout Muslim history has continued to be a vital part
of the religious life and thought of the masses. Despite the
high monotheism which is basic to Islam, this popular level of
religion in the Muslim ethos has served as a foundation upon

which much of the religious life of the Islamic world has rested.

The acceptance by Muhammad of the line of revelation recounted in the Jewish scriptures, and his incorporation of the monotheism of the Hebraic-Jewish tradition into the Koran attest to the great dependence of Islamic doctrine upon Judaism. The Prophet's early attempts to come to an understanding with the Jewish community in Medina are further evidence that he conceived his message as being related to the Jewish religion, and not in complete opposition to it. The fact that the Muslim interpretation of Judaism is its own, and that in many points it runs counter to the Jewish view of Hebraic-Jewish religion does not alter the fact of the close relationship between Judaism and Islam, and the dependence of Islam upon Judaism.

So too, the relationship between Islam and Christianity is a vital factor when one seeks to come to an adequate understanding of the basic theological view-point which characterizes the religious insights of the Koran and early Islam. Viewing itself as being the "crown" or fulfilment of both Judaism and Christianity, Islam gave a place in its thought to the prophetic revelation of "Jesus the son of Mary." In fact, some of the references in the Koran to Jesus, if taken by themselves, would appear to give more honor to the person of Jesus than that accorded to the Prophet Muhammad himself.

In a later discussion of the theological conflict between religions we shall have the opportunity to indicate the close relationship between Islam and its two sister Semitic religions. At this point it is only necessary to be aware of the relationship, and at the same time to warn against the Christian tendency to dismiss Islam's religious uniqueness by classifying it simply as a Christian heresy. The history of Islam gives dynamic denial to any attempt to belittle the inner essence of the religious insights of Muhammad himself or the great figures of the religious life of the Muslim world.

A. ISLAM: THE ENCOUNTER WITH THE PRESENT

If we attempt to discuss other religions in a fashion similar to our treatment of Christianity we shall discover that the leading religions of the world are facing problems in different degree and varying guise; but the problems are nevertheless of like nature and the same demanding urgency.

Islam, also, finds itself confronted by a spirit of the times which is often in open contradiction to Islam as it has existed in the past and as it conceives its mission in the present. To a large degree this spirit of things which exists in the greater part of the world today may be classed as secularism and the attitude which it espouses in the realms of physical science, philosophy, human values, and community living. For many, this secularism is simply Western civilization in its materialistic emphasis and its many-sided expressions in the fields of political economy, applied science, critical scholarship, and attitudes toward the meaning of human existence. While this is certainly true in a large measure, yet we are wide of the mark if we conceive this spirit of the times to be only a creature of the Western world. The Western world through its dynamic expansion into all geographic areas has furnished the impetus to the creation of this spirit, and has had a part in the shaping of its nature, but the spirit itself is not alone Western. It is universal in that it reflects the attitude of world-wide humanity awakening to new visions of life. This awakening in each area of the world reflects the total history, experience, and insights of a common humanity. It is regional in that it is closely bound with the peculiar history and nature of separate areas and their peoples.

It must be made clear that the awareness of the tension between religion and the spirit of the times generally is limited in the Muslim countries to the small portion of the population which by education or occupation has been exposed to the conflict. For many Muslims the conflict does not exist because they themselves have either not been subjected to it in anything other than a peripheral way, or their ability to perceive it has not been developed to the point that they are able to recognize the gulf between the religion which they accept and the way of life and thought which is invading their world. The extent to which an illiterate person of the masses is able to participate in some way in modern industrial, commercial, or community life without being aware of the dual world in which he lives is a constant amazement to the student of mankind. This is true in backward areas and among uneducated people in any section of the world—East or West.

Islam has lived as a close neighbor of the West throughout its history. As a result of its military conquests and its cultural attainments it has left its mark upon the West, while at the same time it has opened itself to the invasion of Western thought and culture. Similarly, geographically situated as a bridge between the West and the East it has not been impervious to the influence of the thought and culture of the East. As a religion this has meant that it has reflected both Eastern and Western religious insights and currents of thought, while as a cultural area overlapping into both it has participated in the strengths and weaknesses found in each.

However, this is not to say that the Muslim area of the world is to be considered simply as a mixture of the East and the West without any structure or content which is uniquely its own. It is difficult to establish objectively that which is essential and different within any one religion which distinguishes it from all other religions, no matter which religion is under consideration. Each religion possesses aspects of thought and worship which are to be found in other religions, and each through the course of its history has been influenced by religious currents which have arisen outside itself. Yet every religion is singular in that the peculiar clustering and arrangement of its thought, the basic presuppositions upon which it is erected, the emphasis it places upon the nature of the Divine, the place it gives to its founder—

these cannot be identified strictly with the total content of another religion. So, too, with Islam.

Nevertheless, because of this close relationship with the rest of humanity, the Islamic world is now caught up in the tensions which are facing mankind as a whole. At the same time, due to its own geography, history, and theological character it is facing problems which are peculiarly its own.

When one leaves the Western world he is immediately struck by the degree of racial, linguistic, and cultural consciousness which is evident among non-Western peoples today. It is difficult to determine to what degree the peoples of the West have gone beyond national or provincial consciousness at the present time, and it must be admitted that the political-military history of this century does not indicate that nationalistic consciousness in its most violent forms has disappeared in the West. However, it probably may be said that in the West there is a growing awareness that nationalism is but a stage in human history and development—a state which must soon be surpassed as history unfolds.

In the non-Western world the situation is markedly different, and in the Muslim world, in particular, the development of nationalistic consciousness in the various areas which go to make up Islam is at a stage experienced by the West decades ago. Processes in this development which were able to evolve over centuries in the West are being forced by present historical circumstance to work themselves out in a few decades. The dim awareness among the intelligentsia of something beyond nationalism, limited as it is, serves as an added spur to the development of nationalism in order that these areas may be on an equal footing with the previously developed national states of the West.

For Islam the religion, the emergence of nationalism as a central factor of thought and political division presents problems of grave magnitude. From its earliest days Islam has conceived of itself as a religion which is supra-regional in character. Viewing the political organization of society as being but an expression of the theological basis of that society, and convinced that all within the theological sphere of Islam are united into one indivisible unity, individualistic and devisive provincial-nationalistic movements have been foreign to the ideal Muslim theory of the state. Of course, separate political entities have existed within Muslim history, but they have been political sub-divisions for the purpose of local government, or expressions of the political ambitions of individual dynasties or theological-political parties, and not, with a few exceptions, assertions of a nationalistic consciousness on the part of the common people who constituted those divisions. At least, they have not challenged the Muslim theological conception of ideal unity among the peoples of Islam in anything like the decisive manner which the modern nationalistic state is now doing.

The Muslim conception of the ideal state is that of theocracy. In the eighteenth and nineteenth centuries this theocratic principle expressed itself in opposition to the then evident distinction which could be made between the Ottoman Empire with its head identified with the Caliphate, and the ethical Islam of the Koran. The Wahhabi movement both in its earliest stages and its present expression in Saudi Arabia, is not a denial of the unity of the Islamic world and of the theocratic ideal. On the contrary, it is an insistence upon them in opposition to the separation of political-social custom and practice from the ideals and teachings of the Koran. Thus one element in the breakup of the political unity of the Islamic world has been the theocratic principle itself as it has objected to political unity which has not been based upon a theological-ethical purity which is in conformity to the foundations of the Faith.

However, orthodox Islam has been united to the political governments of the past at least in principle. This has meant that Islam as a religion, like most religions in their orthodox expressions, has been officially united in its opposition to revolutionary political movements even when those movements have been attempts to bring the state more into line with certain interpretations of the koranic ideal. As a result, Islam has been in tension in the past century with those forces within Muslim society which were seeking to bring about the downfall of the combined Ottoman Empire and Caliphate, while at the same time enlightened groups within Islam have insisted upon the necessity of that very downfall.

In conjunction with the breakup of what was at least a pretense of a united Islam in the form of the Ottoman Empire, the conception of individual national states on the Western pattern emerged. Both the dissolution of the one and the growth of the other were interacting processes which were at work for over a century; with the conclusion of the First World War they became concrete realities in the life of the Muslim world. The people of the Islamic area entered vigorously into the task of erecting national states both as a means of protection from Western colonialism and as a medium for self-expression. In doing so, they were caught in a tension between their desires and needs on the one hand, and the ideal form of political society of their religious heritage on the other.

It is important to note that theocratic emphasis and nationalism are not in complete opposition to one another. The great Muslim thinker of the nineteenth century, Jamāl al-Dīn al-Afghāni, while calling for a purified theocratic state based on the koranic ideal, expressed himself in terms of a nationalism. But, this nationalism ideally was to be Pan-Islamic in character, and not regional. The appeals to national pride and to national unity were on the basis of a nation much greater in scope than individual groupings of people on geographic or ethnic grounds.

The conflict of Islam with the movement of nationalism in the Muslim world of today is the expression of a tension between the concept of ultimate loyalty to the Faith, and the unity of all who submit themselves to the Faith, with political sub-divisions which demand loyalty of their members. The requirement of loyalty to the state which is characteristic of nationalism may not at the moment appear to be in direct opposition to loyalty to Islam and, indeed, it does not appear so to many devout Muslims. However, Islam now finds itself faced with a situation similar to that confronting Christianity. Does the existence within its sphere of separate and possibly competing national states adhere to the injunctions of the Koran and Islamic tradition concerning the political organization of Muslim peoples?

Such a conflict is subtle in nature, and is often only apparent to the theological thinker and the religious leader. The average man is neither aware of such things nor concerned with them. Caught up in the spirit of the times he is called upon to give loyalty to his state and to his religion, oblivious to the contradiction in which he is involved, while the theologians of the Faith seek desperately to bring the two conflicting loyalties into harmony.

In close relationship to this conflict within the Islamic community there is tension and rivalry between religion and the general forces of secularism in the field of education. The Muslim conception of education has been centered around the Koran and the view of the Koran held by the Faith. Holding the Koran to be a divinely written instrument containing within itself all truth, Islam has logically concluded that the highest and only true form of education is knowledge of the Koran. This knowledge has not been in the form of critical study or the application of the rational faculty of man to its content; rather, it has consisted in memorization of it and of the accepted orthodox interpretations applied to it.

With the introduction of Western forms of education and the resultant critical methodology and spirit, there has arisen within Islam a select younger generation which has not been satisfied with the usual and accepted methods of Muslim education for itself, nor for the younger generations of its compatriots. From this dissatisfaction there has arisen a direct challenge to religious orthodoxy which has shaken and is shaking Islam to its very foundations among the educated peoples of the Muslim world. Caught in the necessity of allowing the new education to spread if it is to meet the challenge of the civilization and technology of the West, Islam is at the same time acquiescing in the spread of a spirit which some would hold to be in direct contradiction to itself and its traditions.

In the midst of this conflict with secular nationalism and education, and as a result of the general spirit which they engender, Islam, in company with Christianity, is having to face the challenge of modern science. If the Koran is all that orthodoxy holds it to be, what then of the judgments of science concerning the origin and nature of the world? If the scientific view of things is accepted, as it would appear that it must be if the Muslim world is to play its full part in the modern and future world, does this mean that the strict orthodox conception of the Koran must be abandoned? Are not the two views, the scientific and the koranic, irreconcilable; and would it not seem that the spirit of the times demands that the latter be given up in favor of the former?

One of the most fascinating trends in Islam within the last century has been that of the appearance of various thinkers who have sought by one means and another to reconcile the two views of existence. These attempts at reconciliation have been required to recognize the claims of science and in so doing they have automatically challenged the orthodox interpretation of the nature of the Koran. In the main, they have sought to make the claim that the Koran is not contradictory to the truths established by reason; it reveals ultimate Truth itself and seeming contradictions between it and scientific truth are apparent rather than actual. Further, passages in the Koran which deal with these matters must be understood in a metaphorical sense, or if that does not suffice, they must be studied further in order that their correct meaning might be fully comprehended. Such attempts at reconciliation have rooted upon the firm belief that the Koran, if seen correctly, does not contain falsehood and, further, that truth arrived at by reason cannot contradict Truth revealed by the direct act of the Divine.

Underlying this attempt and the conflict from which it arises is the theological problem of the relation between revelation and reason with which we shall be concerned later. How-

ever, it is necessary at this juncture that it be mentioned in
order that it be understood that much of the conflict between
Islam and the contemporary spirit has its origin in this problem. After early theological struggles in which this problem
was central, Islam cast its lot in favor of the total supremacy
of revelation as over against reason. Now that it is engaged
in a conflict in which human reason is making its claims to
recognition, and making them in a manner which cannot be
ignored, Islam is being forced to adjust itself to the claims.
However, it is not prepared to accept them uncritically. At
the moment it is allowing the claims of reason only insofar as
they can be justified in the light of the traditional source of
authority, though at least for some that authority itself is to
be interpreted by the reason which seeks to be justified.

B. ISLAM: THE INTERNAL TENSIONS

The general impression is prevalent in the West that Islam,
or Muhammadanism as it is more often called, is an organic
institutional unity. Only those who have studied Islam or the
history of the Near and Middle East are aware that Islam also
has its religious divisions, denominations, and sects. The
Muslim emphasis upon the unity and brotherhood of the
Faithful has given to those who do not know the impression
that the religion of Muhammad has not experienced the divisions which Christianity has undergone in its history. However, the conception of unity on the part of Muslims themselves is analogous to the situation in Christianity wherein
Christians speak of the unifying bond of the Faith and the
brotherhood of those who follow Christ. Such a belief is not a
denial of the existence of divisions; it is a deep consciousness
of a unity which rises above the separate factions.

The Muslim world and the Islamic religion are made up of
divergent peoples each possessing a separate history and culture. They are peoples who possessed a history, culture, and
religion of their own before they were brought into the sphere
of Islam. Therefore, they have not been and are not dependent
exclusively upon the norms, customs, and world-view which

are associated with Islam and its Arabic origins. In the sphere of religion this has meant that a complete uniformity of theological belief has not resulted by the simple acceptance of the Faith and the teachings of the Koran. The religious uniformity has been in the nature of the acceptance of basic presuppositions and doctrines. It has not automatically resulted in detailed consistency at all levels of either theological belief or practice in worship.

The two great divisions within Islam, the Sunni and the Shia, have often been compared to the Roman Catholic and Protestant divisions in Christianity. This is only a comparison for the purpose of elementary understanding and is dangerous if carried beyond the fact that both religions are composed of two large groups of believers who may loosely be said to belong to one of the two classifications. The Sunni are those members of the Muslim community who have generally accepted and held to the basic beliefs and "Pillars" of the Faith as they were early developed in the Arabic and western areas of Islam. The Shia, or Shi'ites, are those adherents to the Faith who originally split with the orthodox over the succession to the Caliphate, and who in subsequent times have absorbed into their theology beliefs which may generally be associated with the Persian-Zoroastrian area of the Muslim world. At the present time it would not be correct to make a definite line geographically between the two groups, for during the centuries of Muslim history they have spread and existed throughout the Islamic world. However, for purposes of simplicity it may be said that the Sunni are more closely associated with the central and western areas of Islam, while the Shia are to be found in Persian and eastern Islam.

Generally speaking, Sunni Islam has been that which has been known by the average Westerner who has had any knowledge at all of the Muslim religion. Placing great emphasis upon the Koran as *the* revealed word of God (Allah), and consciously endeavoring to be true to the early view of the Faith held by the Companions or associates of Muhammad, Sunni Islam generally has set itself against innovations of thought and practice within the Faith. The ideal has been the preservation of the "pure" Faith revealed to the Prophet and preserved in the Koran. It is hardly necessary to point out that there is room for great debate as to whether such a purity has been maintained, but nevertheless, in the Sunni mind it has been the function of orthodoxy to strive for such a preservation.

Due to this emphasis and to the comparative simplicity of the original tenets of the Faith, the average Sunni Muslim has been able to limit the required beliefs and worship practices of Islam to the point where his religious faith has been easily adaptable to his daily life in a degree which has not challenged him to disturbing theological thoughts. Accepting the role of the prophet, the truths of the Koran, and the early fundamental interpretations of both, he has been a part of a religion which has buttressed his life and given him a sense of security and fellowship. And, most important in the contemporary situation, he has been given a sense of loyalty to the orthodox interpretation of the Faith which serves to heighten the sense of conflict with those factions which openly deviate from the prevalent conception of orthodoxy.

The rift which resulted in the beginnings of Shia Islam originated over the succession to the Caliphate in the very early years of Muslim history. The partisans of Ali, the cousin and son-in-law of the Prophet, claimed that he was the legitimate successor of Muhammad as Caliph and that the Caliphs in power between the Prophet and Ali were usurpers. In the main, their contention was based upon a hereditary conception of the Caliphate which in time gave rise to the belief that Ali was the possessor of something more than human nature. Highly influenced by Zoroastrian-Persian religious ideas, and probably also by Jewish-Christian conceptions of the Messiah, the Shia belief concerning Ali and his descendants blossomed into a reverence, and in some instances worship, for descendants of the Prophet which has given a much different complexion to Shia Islam than that to be found in Sunni thought and belief.

Coupled with this entrance into Islam of a messianic concept there have arisen throughout the centuries many beliefs which have incorporated religious thought which is certainly foreign to the rather simple doctrines of early Arabic orthodoxy. The strict monotheism of the orthodox position has been qualified by the various representations of Allah or his power which have been allowed in Shia thought. To be sure, the Shi'ites have been able to find a basis for such innovations by their own interpretations of the great variety of thought which is to be found in the Koran, but they cannot dismiss lightly the charge that in so doing they have created a syncretistic religious faith which is not easily identified with the stern and simple religious teachings of Muhammad.

A third division within Islam which historically has cut across the previously mentioned groups is that of Sufism, the Muslim expression of religious mysticism. Many of the great figures in Muslim religious history have either been Sufis or have been highly influenced by Sufi thought. At the present time the mysticism of Islam does not give rise to separate groups within the Faith as it once did in the past. It is a cause for conflict only in the most subtle realms of theology and has declined as a source of the many brotherhoods which once were an important factor in the Muslim world.

Throughout its history Islam has been the scene of the rise of many small religious groups which, like the sects of Christianity, have felt themselves to be the expressions of fundamental religious truths which are being ignored by the Faith as a whole. Due to its emphasis upon the divinely ordained leader this has been true especially within Shia Islam. Such groups have arisen around the figure of an individual religious leader who has claimed to be the possessor of the "Divine Light" which was in Ali, and who has been accepted as either the Messiah (Imam or Madhi) or his forerunner. From such beginnings various sectarian groups have arisen, some of them to die out in time and some to continue as separate bodies within the Faith.

Previous mention has been made of the Wahhabi movement

in its political role in Islam. Tied as it has been in its history
to various political aspirations, many have been tempted to
dismiss it as being simply a factional movement using its theological basis as a rallying point for political purposes. However, as a religious group within Islam it presents a challenge
to the Faith as a whole which cannot be ignored, and which is
a source of tension. Insisting upon a puritanical and rigid
interpretation of Islam on the basis of the Koran, the Wahhabi
movement is in conflict with those who would adopt ways of
life which run counter to the stern moral injunctions of early
Arabic Islam. Situated at the heart of the Islamic world and
in control of the holy city of Mecca, it declares itself in
violent opposition to those who would modernize Islam. As a
reforming influence in the theological and ethical spheres of
Islam, it is a modern expression of the puritan strain of early
Arabic Islam.

It is essential to recognize that the presence of separate
groups within the larger body of the Faith is cause for conflict within Islam not only because of the divergent theological
positions they may hold, but also because of the Muslim conception of the identity of the Faith with political society, to
which we have referred. That is to say, the state in Muslim
theory is the organized political expression of the Faith in
the community. Therefore, if a group within the community
holds that the governing body of society is not in accord with
the "true" teachings of the Koran, it then follows that that
group must seek for the overthrow of the "false" representatives and rulers of Islam. Traditionally, religion has been the
source of political conflict in the Muslim world as it has in the
Christian, or, at least, it has served as the rallying point for
political ambitions.

At the present time Islam has not completely escaped from
this tradition and all that it implies in modern national states
which seek to be representative of all the people within their
borders, and which do not consider themselves to be charged
with the duty of purging the Faith of all who may be charged
with heresy. With the exception of Turkey there is no Muslim

state which may be said to approach closely the Western conception of the secular national state. Conflicts between rival groups which might on the religious plane be purely theological in nature are easily carried over into the political realm because each group considers itself to be the "true" Islam. And to the Muslim mind the areas of religion and society are identical. Of course, the interests of the individual national states, and the pattern of Western nationalism which is being copied does not allow the sectarian religious conflict to be carried over into the political realm as it once was, and it is likely that in the future such conflicts will be even fewer. However, as long as the theory of the state and its ultimate dependence upon and identity with Islam the religion is a central part of Muslim theory, just so long will religious differences within Islam be sources of conflict beyond what the West has come to consider the sphere of religion.

In contradistinction to what has been said in our discussion of the conflict within Islam that arises from the presence of different religious groupings and sects, it remains to be pointed out that underlying all religious division and conflict there is throughout Islam a strong conception of the great brotherhood of Muslims. This brotherhood extends to all who "submit" to the Faith. Coupled with this is the traditional Muslim view that each individual has certain rights of decision in the sphere of religion as long as he remains within the accepted bounds of the religious thought of the community. Where over the course of time certain differences have been accepted as being allowable by tradition and by the consensus of community thought and practice, they do not contribute to conflict with the community in an open manner. They are then, at the most, sources of theological tension and not openly disruptive forces within the body politic.

C. ISLAM: THE VARIETY OF THOUGHT

In the foregoing discussions we have already indicated some of the theological tensions and conflicts which are present in contemporary Islam. The unity of a religion with the under-

lying theological doctrines upon which it rests means that in
its activities in many spheres at every point of conflict in those
activities, theological thought is involved. As we have noted
in the case of Christianity, theology is in conflict with those
beliefs which are in contradiction to it. Very often it is engaged in struggle with the ethos which surrounds it. Being
a living organism within that ethos, and not existing in a
world set apart, it inevitably follows that theology finds itself
in conflict and tension with aspects of thought and life which
are a part of itself. While it is true that in every religion
theology *per se* tends to disassociate itself from the daily life
which exists around it, yet that separation can never be
complete without extinction resulting for the theology. The
demands of living the Faith are constantly pressing upon the
theological constructions of the religion. The degree to which
the theology and theologians of the religion are sensitive to
and involved in the mundane struggles and concerns of the
Faith determines the extent to which the theology is vital and
determinative in the growth and activities of the Faith.

In the case of Islam the tensions within the Muslim world
are involving Muslim theology in internal conflicts which
arise in those areas in which varying theological opinions arise.
In a limited degree the accepted orthodox theology of the past
is no longer secure in its position; it is facing attacks from
within the Faith by those who conceive the present problem
and task of Muslim theology to be the articulation of the
Faith in terms which are applicable to the many problems
which are being faced by the Islamic peoples in the contemporary world. These attacks have been made, in the main, by
the small number of Muslims who are both theologically concerned and alive to the issues which confront modern Islam.
They are not, as yet, and probably will not be in the immediate future, the conscious concern of the vast body of Muslim
peoples.

As in other religions which we shall discuss, Islam is involved in conflict with the levels of the Faith which do not
measure up to the higher religious insights of Islam. Even

without the challenge of the present time, it would be incumbent upon Islam to seek by every legitimate means to purify itself from within. This process of purification, spurred on as it is today by external forces as well, brings Islam face to face with its own theological foundations. The prevalent tendency of the masses of any religion to hold fast to beliefs in the supernatural and miraculous presents a problem for any attempt to lift a religion to levels of belief which are in accord with modern and scientific views of the world. As we have indicated, Islam in many areas is not far removed from pre-Islamic primitivism which still expresses itself in crude animism and superstition. If Islam allows itself to be associated in the popular mind with this level of religious belief, will not Islam share the fate of those beliefs as they are destroyed eventually by modern science and the technical life which appears to lie in the future for even the agricultural peoples of the world? Further, it is not simply a matter of self-defense in the struggle of religion for existence in the new world which is emerging; for Islam it is also a concern that the highest and best of its tradition and religious insights be preserved and made active in the life of its people.

The conflict of Islam with this aspect of religion in its midst is heightened by the fact, previously mentioned, that in the Koran support is given to a view of the nature of existence which coincides with the popular superstitions. The seventh-century Arabic conception of the nature of the world and the forces which operate in it was not one which denies the occurrence of events within the natural realm which are to be explained only by the intervention of supernatural powers. On the contrary, it viewed the realm in which man lives as being continually the scene of the capricious operation of Allah. If the Koran which supports such a world-view is to be upheld by Muslim theology as being the final and true revelation of Allah, is not Muslim theology as a result insolubly wedded to the most fanciful explanations and interpretations of events within the physical world?

This brings us to what is, perhaps, the most profound con-

flict of Muslim theology today; the conflict which is brought
to the fore by the attempts of some Muslim thinkers to adjust
the modern scientific interpretation of the universe to the
Koran, or vice versa. The attempts of individual thinkers and
apologists in this direction are too involved and numerous to
recount in our brief consideration. For the most part they
have consisted of efforts to maintain the ultimate superiority
of the Koran as the final and true revelation of Allah, while at
the same time recognizing the validity of the modern scientific method and its insights into the nature of the world.
These attempts, by one means or another, have argued that
either the Koran must be understood in a metaphorical manner or that its Truths are of such an ultimate nature that even
the truths of science are but beginning approaches to the supreme Truth which it contains.

Such theological-philosophical speculation runs into grave
problems because Islam does not at the present have the
benefit of years of critical scriptural study as does Christianity.
Interpretations which cannot be justified on anything but the
most flimsy grounds are accepted without question by many
Muslim scholars. The works of the leading apologists of Islam
during the past century are filled with interpretations of the
Koran and of Muslim tradition which are not acceptable to
even the most impartial non-Muslim scholarship. The view
of the nature of the Koran held by the vast majority of Muslim
scholars and theologians does not allow them to engage in
the very thing that more and more of them are seeking to do.
They are involved in a conflict from which there is no escape
until they are prepared to accept a radically different view of
the nature of the materials with which they are working, and
to do so would involve them in a break with the past which
at the present time is unthinkable for the great bulk of
Muslims.

A further source of conflict within Muslim theological
thought arises from fundamental Muslim teachings concerning the nature of Allah and the nature of man. While we shall
be concerned in detail with these in a later chapter, they are

of particular concern to us at the moment since they run counter to Western scientific views of causality. Also, they make man a creature so limited in ability and potentiality of self-development that he would seem to be ill suited to the role he must play in modern technical society. Despite claims to the contrary, most theological systems have failed to give adequate intellectual answers to the problems which arise from a belief in an omnipotent deity, and for Islam this problem is made more difficult because of the Muslim belief that Allah is continually involved in every happening within the realms of time and space. All that happens is the result of the pre-determined will of Allah; no event in the material sphere may be said finally to be determined by previous happenings in the empirical world since the will of Allah and not the earlier events determines each new occurrence and its nature. Of course, leading thinkers in Muslim history have developed philosophical-theological systems which have lifted this view above the elementary level in which we have just described it, but the fundamental view is still present challenging all attempts of present apologists and theologians to harmonize the traditional Muslim theology with modern views of existence.

The conflicts which we have indicated, and others which will become apparent in a later discussion of the basic presuppositions of the world's religions, all suggest that one of the urgent tasks facing Islam at the present time is in the area of its theological construction. The proper function of theology in any religion is to lead the way in the articulation of the religious insights of the Faith in the various areas of human concern. If Islam is to meet the challenge of the world today, and the needs of its millions of adherents, it must enter into a period of theological speculation similar to that which produced the Golden Age of Islamic culture and religion in the Middle Ages.

II. *RELIGION*

IN THE EAST

Any discussion of religion in the non-Western world is immediately confronted by the difficulty of bringing into clear and precise focus a large body of belief and practice which by its very nature defies exact classification and exposition. It is especially difficult for the Western mind, accustomed as it is to structure and form in religion, to comprehend such religions as Hinduism and Buddhism with their lack of clear-cut institutional forms and theoretical systematization. Western scholars in their endeavor to force these religions into molds understandable to non-Eastern minds have all too often lost the essence of the religion by their application of Western structure to religions which lie outside such structure.

Hinduism and Buddhism do not share with the Western religions the conception of uniformity of thought as being basic to membership within the religious body. And, even more important, they do not have a notion of a religious body, church, or fellowship which can be made to fit into the Christian pattern of Church and membership within the Church. It is extremely disturbing to the Christian investigator of these religions to discover that when he seeks for articles of faith, or dogmas of belief, with few exceptions he is searching for something which does not exist. If he goes further and seeks to determine the beliefs which are required of the adherent to these religions, he discovers that belief and participation in the religion are not related or dependent upon one another to the degree they are in the West.

Thus, the non-Easterner who seeks to understand the religious situation around the world must at the very outset reconcile himself to the fact that the categories which he is forced to use in his efforts to come to understand Eastern religions are categories which are for the purpose of understanding, and not necessarily correct and actual classifications which would be acceptable to the religions themselves. The Eastern religions very early discovered that religion, at least in its beliefs and theological construction, suffers when it is put into the strait jacket of precise formulations which must be adhered to *in toto*; they generally have not been aware of the dangers which such looseness of theological construction invites. In the past this lack of a clear conception of orthodoxy has served as a strength for Hinduism in particular as it has had to struggle with other religions in India, and for Buddhism it has strengthened its ability to penetrate into areas far from its place of origin. But in the case of both religions that which is a strength has also been a weakness as demonstrated by their difficulty in resisting the forces of well-organized and strictly systematized foreign bodies of religious belief.

Not only is the Western investigator of religion entering into a religiously foreign world when he enters the realm of Eastern religions, he is also penetrating into an unfamiliar ethos of values and methods of reasoning. The Western religious conception of truth and value has been considered to be the norm by which any standards of truth and value are to be judged. This is the natural result of any system of thought and philosophical-theological speculation which conceives its conclusions to be more than simply human judgments. For the Western mind there is at least the possibility of a clear differentiation being made between truth and untruth, between value and disvalue. Therefore, when that mind enters into a world of thought which is unlike its own it concludes that the same standards which it has applied to its satisfaction in its own ethos will be equally applicable in the new surroundings.

It is at this point that the greatest misunderstandings arise between theologians and philosophers of the West and the East. It is but natural for the Western mind to insist that "truth is Truth," while to the Eastern mind such a statement may very well be meaningless and be constructed on the questionable metaphysical assumption that there is an existent eternal Truth which can be ascertained by man and which is apprehensible in terms which differentiate it from something which is non-Truth. We are here caught in the midst of the basic presuppositions of the two worlds of thought—presuppositions which arise out of the very central fabric of the Western and Eastern world views. It is not a simple matter to brush aside twenty-five hundred years of intellectual endeavor and methodology in either of the two areas and thereby to arrive at a mutually acceptable basis for philosophy, theology, or metaphysics. Here lies one of the greatest challenges to the present-day student of philosophy and religion—the attainment of an empathy into the thought world of the East or the West, whichever is not his own.

The locale in which the Eastern religions find themselves is one which at the present time is being subjected to great strains and innumerable tensions. Caught in the inexorable expansion of Western civilization and technology, the Eastern world is undergoing changes at a pace inconceivable a few generations ago. The decisions which are being forced upon the East are made even more portentous by the speed in which they must be made. No longer is the man of the East free to make choices leisurely between what aspects of Western civilization or technology he will incorporate into, or reject, from his own way of life. He is caught up into the maelstrom of foreign ways which are invading his world with a rapidity and force against which he has little resistance. Even with the attainment of his own political independence in some areas, he has not escaped the necessity of immediate choice which is forced upon him. In fact, the attainment of political independence, accompanied as it is by the development of local nationalism on the Western pattern, has increased rather than lessened the challenge of Western civilization.

The choice before the Eastern world is not simply the alternative between accepting or rejecting Western civilization and material advantages. The East is rapidly discovering that the adoption of simple technological machines means also the opening of itself to more subtle aspects of culture which strike at the very heart of the whole of Eastern life and thought. The adoption of Western dress is not a mere matter of changing the cut of the cloth which drapes the body; it results in a subtle alteration of the thought processes of the individual who makes such a change. It does not make the individual a Westerner, but it does qualify some of the ingrained Eastern attitudes which go to make up the individual personality.

The Eastern world is discovering that, as it eagerly opens its arms to the material technological advantages which are obvious in Western civilization, it is also making itself vulnerable in the areas it holds most dear—its culture and its religion. The subtle, almost imperceptible ties between a people's cultural-spiritual ethos and their material ways of life are now vividly apparent to the discerning man of the East. He is coming to realize that the development of a civilization in the Western pattern implies the rejection of at least some basic aspects of the world view which is his heritage.

The predominant religions of the East, Hinduism and Buddhism, are inextricably bound with the totality of culture and society as it has existed for centuries in the Eastern world. Any weakening of the culture, any change in the social structure, implies a weakening and a change in their power and their form. The struggles and adjustments which the adherents of these religions are having to make in the realms of agriculture, commerce, technology, government, and education are struggles from which Hinduism and Buddhism cannot remain aloof. The adjustments which are being made in such areas of life are forcing both religions to see the necessity of adaptation on their part if they are to maintain a close relationship with their adherents.

To speak generally of the two religions, both Hinduism and Buddhism have undergone a series of reactions in the past decades as they have been confronted by the encroaching civilization, culture, and religion of the West. There have been those adherents of the religions who under the stimulus from the West have sought to *reform* their native religion. These individuals while conscious of the values of their own religion, have also been aware that Hinduism or Buddhism needed reforming if they were to be true to their own essence, let alone meet the challenge of Western religion. In most cases these attempts at reform have adopted in one fashion or another certain theological or organizational aspects of Christianity. They have sought to restore the Eastern religion to what the reformers considered to be its true and proper nature, and in bringing about this restoration they have adopted values and methods which they discerned in Western religion.

In addition to reform movements within the two great Eastern religions there have been impulses toward *revival* wherein the attempt is being made to revive the religion not so much by means of reform as by appealing to the religious loyalty and sensitivity of the adherents of the religion. These revival movements have sought to overcome the lethargy of the individual Hindu or Buddhist by reminding him of the values which are present in his religion, and by appealing to his sense of pride in that which is his own heritage. At this point the growing sense of nationalism in the countries of the East, and the natural desire of a people to be loyal to that which is peculiarly their own has aided and is aiding the resurgence of both Hinduism and Buddhism particularly in India and in the Southern Buddhist countries.

Reform and revival, coupled with the challenge of Western religion and civilization, have led to *renaissance*. In the case of each of the two religions this has been marked by the rebirth of interest in the traditional art, the literature, the theology-philosophy, and the basic world view inherent to the religion. Here, also, the new national pride in the heritage of the past has played its part. Coupled with this renaissance, and a fundamental aspect of it, has been the emergence of philosophers and theologians dedicated to the articulation of their culture and religion in terms meaningful to the West. Such men as Professor Radhakrishnan in Hinduism and Professor Suzuki in Buddhism have achieved high rank in the circle of world philosophers by their utilization of the intellectual wisdom of both the East and the West as they have sought to convey the values of Hinduism and Buddhism to the Western mind.

However, a false impression would be left concerning the state of religion in the Eastern world if one other trend were not mentioned. This is the *revolt* from religion which is one of the central factors in the religious life of the East today. To a degree this revolt is a counterpart of the rebellion against religion which occurred earlier among youth of the Western world. However, in the case of the youth of the East it is of a more deep seated nature in that it is not simply a turning away from religion. It involves a rejection of the customs, mores, and culture of the East as well. Anyone who has lived in the East even for a limited period has been struck by the number of young men and women who have not only given up the religion of their fathers, but who in this process have declared their independence of the total heritage of their native land. The fact that total separation from their heritage is impossible has only increased the tragedy, for it has created individuals who in their desire to become Western have only succeeded in being neither Western nor Eastern.

The aforementioned currents and trends within the religious life of the East are indicative of the turmoil in which the Eastern religions find themselves. On the one hand, they cannot be said to be reformed, revived, nor in a state of new life. Neither can they be said to be rejected. Yet nothing would be further from the mark than to come to the conclusion that they are in a state of lethargy near death, quiescently awaiting their destruction at the hands of Western civilization and

Christianity or Islam. All of these currents are present within Hinduism and Buddhism at the present time, and the very fact of their presence indicates the existence of vitality and a potentiality for new life in a degree which they have not known before.

Slowly Hinduism is awakening from the sleep of the last centuries as it finds itself a central part of a new nation which is dreaming great dreams. Faced by the onslaughts of the West in the spheres of material civilization, culture, and religion, it is stirring and searching within itself for resources by which it can resist these pressures. And, most important of all from the perspective of both the East and the West, it is discovering resources which are not only suitable for defense but which are also adaptable for offense against Western religion. It may well be that within the foreseeable future it will be Hinduism which will be challenging Christianity not only in India but in the West as well.

So too, in many areas of Buddhism the period of lethargy and decline is over. The strength of northern Mahayana Buddhism in Japan is made obvious by the renaissance of Buddhist thought which it is bringing to the attention of the theological-philosophical world. Southern Hinayana or Theravadin Buddhism in such areas as Ceylon, Burma, and Thailand is in a period of resurgence as it joins in the new nationalism and revived pride of these peoples. We, therefore, embark upon a survey of these two religions as they participate in the conflict of religions today with the consciousness that we are viewing religions of strength whose potential influence in the religious life of the world in the immediate future must not be minimized.

1. Hinduism in Conflict

Despite the peaceful appearance which it exhibits to the casual observer, Hinduism has been engaged in numerous violent controversies during its long history. There have been struggles with the many local indigenous religions which

cover the whole of the sub-continent of India, as well as conflicts with new Indian religions and invading religions from
outside of India. The seeming phlegmatic character of Hinduism as a whole can easily deceive one into assuming that
Hinduism has continued on its way paying little attention
to her contenders for the spiritual allegiance of Indians. It
would almost appear that Hinduism has proceeded undis-
turbed in the conviction that its powers of absorption would
sooner or later defeat the opponent. While this may be true
to a degree, a closer inspection reveals that with the rise
of each successive contending religion Hinduism has in the
course of time stirred itself and found methods whereby it
has maintained its basic position in the Indian religious
scene.

If we recognize, first of all, the almost impossibility of de-
fining Hinduism in any fashion acceptable either to Hindus
or to non-Hindu scholars we are on the threshold of coming
to an understanding of something of the nature of the conflict
of Hinduism with itself and with its more easily defined
opponents. Composed of a vast heterogeneous mass of beliefs
and practices, Hinduism generally has not considered itself to
be in conflict with other religions in the same manner that,
for example, Christianity and Islam have considered themselves to be in conflict with each other. Ever ready to allow
the most divergent of religious systems a place within its all-
embracing arms as long as such systems would acknowledge
the truth of certain basic Hindu presuppositions, the conflict
of Hinduism with other religions has not been one of an
either/or nature. Hinduism's struggle with non-Hindu religious views is of the nature of *yes/and*. Once its opponents
have made concessions in the direction of allowing the place
and validity of varied approaches to the Divine, from the
Hindu viewpoint the basic reason for conflict has been removed. Hinduism can now leisurely proceed to incorporate
its rival into itself and, in the end, emerge triumphant in the
struggle. In some instances the process has occupied many
centuries, and in a sense it may be said that it is still contin-

uing even in the case of such ancient opponents as Jainism and
Buddhism.

As we shall have occasion to note later, Hinduism in company with the other great religions of the modern world is not
free from numerous divisions within itself. However, to a
remarkable degree these divisions are not looked upon as being of a conflicting nature; rather, they are seen as com-
plementing each other. While we must take account of the
variations of religious thought and practice within Hinduism
and note that these variations do give rise to tensions within
the body of Hinduism, yet it is essential that we understand
that to a large extent they are of a more minor nature than
the conflicts to which we have referred in Christianity and
Islam. On the whole, they do not reflect the attitude of vigor-
ous conflict which religious differences so often exhibit in
the West.

A. HINDUISM: THE ENCOUNTER WITH
THE PRESENT

The conflict of Hinduism with the spirit of the times is a
struggle in which Hinduism is participating along with religion around the world. For Hinduism it is not simply a
struggle between religion and the constantly changing life of
the society of which it is a part. Hinduism is involved in the
struggle which history has forced upon the East as a whole—
the struggle between the traditional way of life and cluster of
values which are particularly Hindu, and the invading
civilization and culture of the West. For Hinduism the
struggle is not one of minor adjustments. It is a conflict between two ways of life and the presuppositions which support
these ways.

The situation is not such wherein Hinduism can make a
simple clear-cut choice between remaining as it has been in
the past, or adopting Western civilization and culture. The
relationships between religion and culture are too decisive for
that. If the Indian people are to continue in their incorporation
of Western technology and ways of life into India as they ap-

pear to be doing at the present time, it is impossible for Hinduism to remain as it has been in the past. For Hinduism to do so would require that it exist completely isolated from the people and society upon which it depends for support. Such a situation would insure that Hinduism as a religion and as a culture would soon disappear from the Indian and world scene.

Furthermore, such a choice is not open to Hinduism. India has embarked upon a political and economic program which, if at all successful, will result in the creation of an Indian nation participating fully in the political and economic affairs of the world. India cannot do this without adopting to a large extent the ways of the West. Indeed, under the guidance of the Congress party and its leaders India has already become, in a measure, Western. True, these leaders envisage an India which will incorporate into itself the best of the West while retaining the best of the native heritage of the past. But even to achieve such a state the challenge is placed squarely before Hinduism that it adjust itself to those features of Western civilization and culture which will be necessary for the Indian state if it is to attain its ambition of being a leading nation of the world.

A primary source of tension between Hinduism and the spirit of the times arises in regard to the concern with physical material betterment which is so central a part of Western civilization, and which is an essential aspect of new India's struggle to become a modern nation. The colleges and universities of India, along with the great Western universities which attract Indian students, are turning out large numbers of Hindu youth who are dedicating their lives to the physical betterment of the Indian people. The legacy of Westernized urban centers created by the British during the last centuries places a constant demand upon modern India that it deal with hygiene, education, and social planning.

All of this is a source of tension because Hinduism in the past has not demonstrated a concern or passion for the physical well being of its adherents. Despite the claims of some modern

Hindu apologists to the contrary, it is of the nature of Hinduism that it set before man as the highest ideal the renunciation of concern with the physical world. When the whole of a society is indoctrinated with the belief that life in the world is something to be escaped, and that escape from it is best attained by unconcern with it, it naturally follows that such a society will not devote a great amount of attention to its physical surroundings.

However, the course of history has brought India into a position where such unconcern and inaction is no longer possible. The youth of India, and the far-sighted leaders of the nation are not content for India to continue in the patterns of the past in this regard. Even the uneducated villager who occasionally sees a Western movie and who is aware of the products of Western technology which more and more intrude into his village life is brought to ask the question as to why these things are not fully his.

This spirit of the times which causes men to look to the material world for rescue from the miseries of life is leading the keener minds of India to devote themselves to science, industry, and social welfare. Thus Hinduism is being deprived of the very minds which in the past turned to theological-philosophical speculation. The full nature of this loss is only realized when it is noted that for many who throw themselves fully into the secular concerns of modern India, their new interests not only imply a break with the traditional Hindu attitude in the matter, but also serve notice of a definite revolt from Hinduism, at least from Hinduism as it has been conceived in the past.

Contemporary Hindu thinkers are extremely anxious to make clear that the traditional doctrine of *maya* concerning the world and its nature is not correctly understood when it is translated as "illusion." There is no doubt but what basically the term as used in Hindu philosophical speculation might better be translated as "secondary reality." However, it cannot be denied that Hinduism through the centuries has placed such emphasis upon the ultimate unimportance of the

physical world and existence in it that the general tone of
Hindu civilization has been one of indifference to endeavor
in the physical realm. Modern intellectual expositions of the
great Hindu epic *The Bhagavad Gita*, or interpretations of the
doctrine of Karma in such a way as to espouse the doing of
acts of service for humanity, do not alter the fact of the Hindu
ethos and its general renunciation of human activity in the
physical sphere.

Further, it must be recognized that Hinduism has been and
is associated with an agrarian form of life, certainly not with
an industrial society. In part the conflict of Hinduism with
the present spirit of things is analogous with the same struggle
on the part of Christianity at the dawn of the Industrial Age
in the West. It may very well be that the analogy will go
further in that the adjustment of religion to society will be of
a similar nature. However, if such an adjustment is to take
place, Hinduism will be forced to concern itself with the
physical world as it has not done before. Gross superstition
in regard to such things as amulets and their powers may be
able to exist in an industrial society, but a religion which
desires to be meaningful in such a society will find it difficult
to encourage such superstition at the same time it meets the
challenges of an industrial age and its problems.

As has been indicated, the youth of India are at the center
of the tension betwen Hinduism and the modern spirit. It
may be that the youth in the village at the present time is not
greatly concerned with the tensions beween his hereditary
religious view of things and the new secular world that is
arising about him. But, the modern Indian nation has no
intention of leaving such youth in their present state. Even
the youth of the most isolated village of the next generation
will be caught up in the stress which is the concern of the
educated urban youth of today.

At the present time the urban and educated youth of India
to a large measure are entranced by Western civilization and
the material advantages it gives them. For some, there is
no recognition as yet as to the break with their culture and

religious ethos which is demanded of them as they participate in these advantages. For others, the issue is clear and they have entered into a whole-hearted revolt against Hinduism and the ethos of India. They are often more British or American in their habits and their attitudes than many young people in the West!

But there is a third group among the youth of India, a group which is more clearly aware of the issues involved and the chaos which results from a rejection of the heritage which is one's own. Clearly discerning the advantages of much of the civilization and technology of the West, they are also cognizant of the weaknesses which are a part of that civilization. Coupled with this they are aware that the adoption by India of much that is Western will demand that the lower superstitious elements within Hinduism be rejected. They are, therefore, turning their backs upon many of the traditional rites and practices which are associated with temple worship, while at the same time they are becoming more firm in their adherence to the Hindu view of life found in the great literature of the past and expounded by the leading philosophical-theological thinkers of the present. However, the problem remains for them as to whether such a world view will support the technology and civilization which they envisage for the India of the future.

B. HINDUISM : THE INTERNAL TENSIONS

Throughout our discussion of the religious situation in the world we have been using the term "conflict" in an attempt to convey forcefully the seriousness of the struggle in which religion is engaged in various spheres of tension. Words which would suggest a less serious situation, or which would merely imply that the religions of the world are in a state of disagreement with each other and with certain aspects of their environment, would fail to indicate with adequate force the seriousness of the state of religion in the world. However, when we consider the struggles within Hinduism it is necessary to soften our terminology. What appears to the non-

Hindu to be conflict within Hinduism, must be recognized as being accepted variety from the viewpoint of Hinduism.

This is not to say that there are not those groups or factions within Hinduism which consider themselves to be more correct in their beliefs or practices than other groups. Nor is it meant to suggest that violent controversy does not occur between differing sects within the Hindu fold. What must be made clear, however, is that the nature of Hinduism is such that Western terms such as "orthodoxy" and "heterodoxy" are often misused when applied to the Hindu religious scene.

Hinduism is in conflict with itself in the sense that within the total body of the religion there are such varieties of belief and practice that to the outsider it would appear that these varieties are totally separate religions rather than participating elements within an integrated whole. In periods of calm it has not seemed to be necessary for Hinduism to seek to bring these groups into a greater unity of thought and practice. At the most such unity could be left to the slowly moving currents which tend to amalgamate divergent beliefs and practices within a related geographic area.

Further, as has been suggested, Hinduism's extremely loose conception of orthodoxy with few exceptions has not caused a consciousness of conflict to be present even in the mind of the religiously active Hindu. There has been little objection on the part of Hinduism as a whole to the emergence of new sects or groups which have placed a particular emphasis upon some aspect of religious belief or practice. Diversity in the realm of religion has been allowed on the basis of the presupposition that the paths to the Divine are many and each man must find the path which is suited to his station in life.

Events of today, however, are challenging the traditional toleration of such great variety within Hinduism. Conscious that the outside world looks upon it as a unity, and that it is judged very often by the lower forms of religious expression which it allows, modern Hinduism is gradually awakening to the need to purify itself. This trend arises from a sincere religious desire for high spiritual attainment as well as from the natural desire of India to present the best possible appearance to the world. The movements of reform and revival which began in the last century, and the contemporary renaissance and resurgence of Hinduism today are highly sensitive to the problem of the lower levels of religion which still stand as blots upon Hinduism as a whole.

Throughout its long religious history India has been the scene of a constant process in which the higher level of Sanskrit Hinduism has sought to impose itself upon the indigenous religions of the various areas and people of India. The process is still in operation. The tribal religion of a people is incorporated into the total Hindu system, their gods are given a place in the pantheon of Hindu deities, and the people receive a status in the social system by being incorporated into the caste structure. However, due to the loose conception of orthodoxy which we have noted, this has not meant that in the course of time the tribal religions have been supplanted by the higher level of Hinduism. To a large degree the tribal religions have remained as they were and the result has been a Hinduism which is less a unified religion and more a conglomeration of religions.

It is true, of course, that all religions share in the problem of the chasm between their higher intellectual complex levels and the lower levels which are to be found among the ignorant and uncultured. Where these two are not separated by an unbridgeable gulf they often serve each other by their interaction. The intellectual calls upon the other to lift its sights to the higher things of the spiritual life; the religion of the common people demands that the other does not lose its heart and its sensitivity in cold unfeeling intellectualism. The problem in Hinduism has been, and is, that the gulf is so wide between the two that a healthy interaction is extremely difficult. Nor has there been the consciousness of the need of such dynamic relationship between the varieties of religious experience and insight which go to make up the total religion.

The Indian nation is now in the midst of a struggle to become a political unity. Racial, linguistic, and cultural differences within India have not been overcome by the years of British rule nor by the sudden achievement of political independence. Discerning leaders in the religious sphere of Indian life are aware that the political-national problem is also a problem for Hindu religion. Maintaining that the new India shall be a secular state offering freedom of religion to all, India's present leadership is also cognizant that a healthy modern Indian state cannot rise out of a religious background or base of such diversity as the present popular Hinduism of the masses.

The processes of education and industrialization will, of course, inevitably lift the lower levels of thought and worship, but the conflict between the high and the low is made more apparent by the same process. The problem for Hinduism is whether in the course of the change those who are uprooted from their religious faith and practice will declare themselves completely independent of religion, or whether Hinduism itself will be able to offer them a higher religious faith which meets their needs.

The sectarian divisions within Hinduism, while convenient to the student of the religion for purposes of understanding, do not reflect dynamically conscious differences in theology or worship among the masses of the people. These divisions are indicative of worship of different deities within Hinduism and of the influence of great religious leaders who themselves have often become deified; they do not represent vital consciously conflicting theologies which are striving in opposition to one another. The average Hindu is not aware of the differences, and even when he occasionally is he does not see them as being causes of conflict.

The most obvious source of conflict and tension within Hinduism at the present time is caste. Caste is the social expression of Hinduism, and as such is closely related to the theological presuppositions upon which the whole of Hinduism rests. There have been many who in endeavoring to define

Hinduism as a religion have defined it as membership in a caste. While from a sociological point of view this definition may be acceptable, and in practice it would be accepted by many Hindus themselves, yet such a definition tends to overlook the fact that caste itself is dependent upon a world view which is Hindu. Hinduism does not grow out of the caste system; rather, the caste system proceeds from Hinduism. The present tendency of some educated Hindus to consider themselves to be free from caste and its restrictions while at the same time they maintain themselves still to be Hindus, is indicative of the fact that we are making a dangerous error if we insist upon a strict identification of membership in a caste and being a Hindu. True, such instances are not yet the general rule in Indian life but they are demonstrating that the breakdown of caste which is taking place in the more Westernized areas of India does not automatically mean that Hinduism itself in its religious role is doomed if caste as it has been known in the past is abolished.

Nevertheless, the one area in which it may be said that Hinduism is engaged in violent conflict with itself is the sphere of caste. The conception of *Dharma* in life—that is, ideal duty in the state of life in which one is born—is a cardinal tenet of Hinduism, and is the authority upon which caste duty and faithfulness to caste membership rests. The individual who revolts from that duty and the caste laws which are put upon him by his birth has inevitably declared himself to be in opposition to the accepted view of Hinduism. The fortunate urban Indian who is able to ignore caste to some extent is forced, if he sincerely wishes to consider himself a Hindu, to construct for himself a view of Dharma which runs counter to the traditionally accepted interpretation of the term.

Hinduism is in conflict with itself at this point in that there is a minority of Hindus of stature and influence in modern India who are challenging the old view of caste. Generally they are not seeking the abolition of caste but, rather, are attempting to change the traditional view of it. The work of

Mahatma Gandhi among the non-caste masses, and his bestowing on them the term "Harijan," or "children of God," is
a case in point. The strict Brahmanic Hindu may frown upon
Gandhi's action, but he cannot escape from the consequences
of it. Influential Hindus who are committed to a lifting of the
conception of caste to a higher level are motivated not only
by the recognition that the old view of caste is incompatible
with the new life which modern India envisages; they are also
conscious that caste as it now is does not measure up to the
high ideal of Dharma which is found in the best writings and
traditions of the past.

Thus it is that Hinduism is caught up into a struggle with
certain aspects of itself. The lower forms of religious life
which cannot be dismissed as being merely peripheral present
a challenge to the leadership of religious and political India.
The conflict and the successful conclusion of it from the point
of view of the educated Hindu is made more difficult because
he is conscious that he is engaged in a struggle with a conception of religion which is part of his own heritage and
persuasion. Conquer he must if Hinduism is to live and to
contribute its resources to a modern India, but in the very act
of conquering, the traditional toleration and open-mindedness
which is essential to Hinduism is called into question.

The tension in the realm of sectarian divisions is a problem
which, though minor at the present time, may well become
more acute in the immediate future as Hinduism is forced to
define itself more precisely. In the violent struggle of modern
times for the political and spiritual allegiances of men each
conflicting claimant must present a united front as it engages
in the conflict. The emphasis of certain evangelistic groups
within Hinduism upon the common basic presuppositions of
the divergent elements within Hinduism is indicative of the
growing awareness of alert Hindus that the unity of Hinduism
must be made stronger and the disunity lessened. And, further,
the modern mind, both Eastern and Western, is not easily
contented with giving allegiance to a body of thought which
lacks coherence and uniformity within itself.

C. HINDUISM: THE VARIETY OF THOUGHT

The grounds for much of the tension and conflict in the realm of thought within Hinduism have been indicated by our previous discussion. It is essential to see that what in the past have been no more than differences of opinion are rapidly becoming more serious in nature, as Hinduism comes more and more to participate in the demands of the present crisis in Indian and Eastern life. No longer can Hinduism smile benevolently upon conflicting theological beliefs as it once did. Modern man, be he Eastern or Western, demands integrity and consistency of thought to a degree unknown in India in the past.

The reform movements within Hinduism during the past century and a half have contributed much to the growing conflict of thought. Spiritually sensitive and brilliant minds within the Hindu fold have found themselves unable to shrug off certain aspects of Western religious thought, both Muslim and Christian. Spurred on by these beliefs which have appeared to them to be superior to the prevailing doctrines in Hinduism, they have incorporated them into their own peculiar religious systems while usually claiming to find such tenets supported in the great Hindu teachings of the past. In so doing they have entered into conflict with the conservative tradition of Hinduism which is on the defensive particularly against the religions which have been associated with military invasion and colonialism. Despite its traditional tolerance of divergent religious thought, Hinduism has not escaped the natural defensive reaction of conservatism in its effort to maintain itself against the varied onslaughts of the West. Many have correctly seen this invasion as being representative of a unified system of life and thought, and have been aware of the danger of assuming that isolated items could be absorbed by Hinduism without causing the decay of the whole of it.

Certain reform movements of the nineteenth century placed themselves in direct opposition to idolatry. Rammohun Roy, in the first decades of the century, struck out vigorously against the place of idols in Hindu worship and argued that those passages in the great religious writings of the past which would appear to support idolatry were intended to be taken in a figurative sense. The great Absolute which is the prime figure in Hindu philosophical-theological thought, he maintained, is formless and should be worshipped as such by all Hindus of whatever stage of life they may be. Roy and his successors, in conjunction with Islam and Christianity, have placed before Hinduism a challenge which cannot be ignored as Hinduism seeks to be meaningful in the life and thought of India today.

Further conflict within the thought of Hinduism is to be seen as the result of the work of another religious leader of the last century, Swami Dayananda Saraswati. Dayananda was more a revivalist than a reformer, and had as his watchword the cry "Back to the Vedas!" However, he also sought for the purifying of those practices and conceptions which he considered to be untrue to the sacred teachings of the ancient Vedic writings. Thus, at the same time he was seeking to protect Hinduism from the invasion of the West he also contributed to conflict within Hinduism by his stern denunciation of much that through the centuries has become a part of Hinduism.

These and other religious leaders during the last century and a half have brought conflict into Hinduism by their attacks upon idolatry, rampant polytheism, non-theism, and the inactivism which has been characteristic of Hinduism in the sphere of ethics. Differing widely in many of their attitudes they have, nevertheless, confronted traditional Hindu religious belief and practice with the challenge of a higher religious thought which they have maintained is to be found within the sources of Hinduism itself.

The disturbances which automatically follow within a body of religious doctrine and custom when leaders from its own ranks challenge its accepted beliefs and ways cannot be dismissed as mere incidents which have no consequences. In the present century the attacks of Mahatma Gandhi upon the traditional views of caste and the indifference of Hinduism to ethical concerns cannot be said to be without its impact. Despite the negative attitude of the more "orthodox" Hindus toward his views and activities, the great body of thinking Hindus find themselves challenged by the vision he has put before them.

This, then, is the conflict. Shall the norms of better and worse in religious thought and practice which are acceptable to the West be allowed to become the norms for Hinduism? As Hinduism becomes more self-critical and turns to its own written sources for guidance in that criticism, how much shall it allow its view of itself to be influenced by the religious standards of the non-Hindu world? And, most important of all, to what degree shall Hinduism demand of its many branches a uniformity of theological belief and practice in worship, in order that it may present a united front in the conflict of today? The answer to such questions which will be given by Hinduism in the decades immediately ahead will have profound significance for both India and the world.

2. Buddhism in Conflict

The religion which originated in the thought and experience of Siddhartha Gautama, the Buddha, has become the religion of a large portion of the world in the twenty-five hundred years since his activities. Conceiving of itself as being universal, and therefore applicable to all mankind, it has spread from its homeland in India to all areas of the East. No longer of any consequence in India, it is the predominate religion in the Far East and in the Southeastern areas of Asia. Vitally alive in some areas, and decadent in others, it presents a conflicting contrast of religious insight and ignorance, subtle thought and superstition, dynamic resurgence and lethargy. Because of this variety we must caution ourselves again that our brief and general discussion will only skim the surface of the involved and long history, theology, and present state of Buddhism.

Buddhism may be described in its origins as a heresy or reform within Hinduism. Its founder came from Hinduism, its early members and leaders were from Hinduism, many of its basic presuppositions were either identical with, or offshoots from, Hindu thought, and its formative years were spent in the Hindu religious and cultural ethos. Due to the nature of its thought and the method of salvation which it preached, it very early assumed the monastic nature which has characterized it throughout its history in most of its expressions. Split into two primary groups over theological matters early in its history, it has continued down to the present day as a two-dimensioned religion which through these two main expressions has dominated the religious and philosophical life of the Far Eastern world.

In the process of its spread over such a vast territory Buddhism has absorbed into itself the local religion and culture of diverse areas which have accepted its message. As a consequence Buddhism has taken on a varied appearance in the separate areas in which it now exists while, at the same time, it has maintained a loose unity which has served to give it a general structure whereby it could be distinguished as a separate and supra-regional religion spreading over the Far Eastern world. Because of its tolerance for variations within religion, Buddhism has taken part in the interesting phenomenon of "dual belonging" in which an individual may be a part of more than one religion, using the values offered by various religions or systems of thought to aid him in the spiritual and ethical problems which face him. Syncretistic in nature in a fashion similar to Hinduism, Buddhism generally has been able to establish itself among various peoples without causing a violent change in their culture or society; yet in the long run of history it has gradually created a culture which may be said to be genuinely Buddhist in most of the areas in which it is found.

An important factor in any consideration of contemporary Buddhism is the variety of strength which is to be found in the Buddhism of separate regional areas. In company with Islam

and Christianity, the other two religions which have conceived of themselves as being universal, Buddhism finds itself
involved in the strengths and weaknesses of the regions in
which it exists. This means that in the present situation the
vitality of Buddhism in any one area is closely bound to the
economic, political, and cultural dynamism present in that
area. It is difficult to determine to what degree the strength
or weakness of Buddhism in a given area is dependent upon
like conditions in other matters in the region, and to what
extent these strengths or weaknesses are indicative of a condition which is exclusively that of the religion. The absence
of vitality in Chinese and Korean Buddhism in the last centuries, for example, has occurred at the same time these
nations have exhibited a general lack of strength in all other
realms of thought and activity. Because of the union of a
religion with the totality of its ethos, is such weakness in
these other spheres a result of the lack of strength of Buddhism, or vice versa? Again, is the present resurgence of
Buddhism in the Southeastern Asian countries simply the
result of their new-found nationalism and cultural pride, or is
this new political strength and cultural vitality the expression
of a dynamic within southern Buddhism?

A. BUDDHISM: THE ENCOUNTER WITH
THE PRESENT

The conflict of Buddhism with the present age and the
spirit of materialism, technology, secularism, and statism is
similar to that of the struggle with the same opponent on the
part of the other of the great religions which we have discussed. As a non-Christian religion existing in an area which
is being invaded by this spirit it is involved in the total
reaction and defense which is being made by the East. The
degree in which this present spirit and developing world way
of life has been and is being adopted by the Buddhist lands
makes it certain that for Buddhism, as for the other religions,
there can be no escape from the problems which this spirit

presents to any religion it encounters. Therefore, much that we have said previously is true in the case of Buddhism.

A fundamental problem for Buddhism in this conflict is the attitude toward the world and existence in it which is basic to Buddhist thought and teaching. Viewing the world and existence as something which is to be escaped if possible, the general Buddhist attitude is in direct conflict with a concern for temporal affairs and material success. This, of course, is the ideal attitude and is not typical of the average layman of the Faith, but it does indicate that ideal Buddhism must seek to adjust itself to the concerns of its adherents in the modern world. Just as the other-worldiness of Christianity must remain in tension with its concern for this world and its problems, so too, Buddhism must endeavor to bring its emphasis upon the ultimate non-existence of the "self" in a sphere outside of the world into a proper and healthy tension with the acknowledged temporal existence of man and his struggles in the earthly sphere.

Buddhism is fortunate in this regard in that the teachings of Gautama himself can serve as a guide in the present conflict. Turning away from the Hindu conception of escape from the world by asceticism and renunciation of the world, the Buddha taught the way of the "Middle Path," a way in which man is charged to view the nature of existence in what Buddhists have always claimed to be a realistic fashion. That is to say, since at the moment man obviously cannot escape from existence, therefore it is wise for him so to exist that the conflicts and sorrows of existence impinge upon him in the smallest degree possible. This has furnished the ideal way of the Buddhist monk and it has been basic to Buddhist thought as a whole.

However, it will immediately be apparent that such a position on the part of a religion will, if taken at all seriously, impregnate a society with an attitude toward life which is not conducive to the activism in the physical world which is demanded by the spirit of the present day. In those areas of

Buddhism where the life of the monk is the ideal, and where every individual believes that in some existence he shall embark upon such a path, this attitude toward existence is a part of society to the extent that Buddhism is by the very nature of things in conflict with the modern spirit.

One of the greatest difficulties for the non-Buddhist at this point is that it is all too easy to conclude that the ideal or theological position of a religion is identical with the beliefs which are held by the average adherents to the religion. If we examine closely the situation in Christianity we realize that the ideals of the Faith influence our approach to life and its problems, they give us a norm from which we can work, but this does not mean that we consciously and necessarily apply these ideas to even the major decisions which we make. Any investigator of Christianity from outside would naturally give emphasis to the Sermon on the Mount as a rich source for the understanding of the Christian ethical ideal, but Christians would be the first to point out that he is in error if he concludes that the Sermon is the workaday principle which is constantly operative in Christian society.

In Buddhism this is also the case. The ease with which certain Western scholars have classified Buddhism as a "world-denying" religion betrays an emphasis upon theological thought to the neglect of the areas of applied religion in which men and women have to live and to work. The Buddhist peoples have not lived through the centuries producing the art and culture which enriches their world as a people who despise the world and its pleasures. In the sphere of actual living they have developed a philosophy of life which has made living both pleasant and satisfying. The basic Buddhist "truth" that existence involves suffering is a theological-philosophical doctrine which lends a certain flavor to the world view of the culture and society; it does not cause men to turn from the pursuits and endeavors of existence any more than the fundamental Christian "truth" about the nature of material possessions causes any sizable number of modern Christians to forsake the pursuit of material security or wealth.

It is necessary that the foregoing be written in order that we perceive the full nature of the conflict in which Buddhism is engaged. If the whole of Buddhist society were committed to the renunciation of the world, which we have wrongly assumed to be the nature of Buddhism at its practical lay levels, then it would be engaged in a decisive struggle in which the issues would be clear. Then we would have a do-or-die conflict between "world-denying" and "world-affirming" views of human existence. However, the issue is not so precisely defined and the struggle, therefore, is of a more complicated nature. The question is whether Buddhism will be able to maintain its hold on the minds and affections of its adherents as they live in the world while that world is more and more challenging the basic assumptions which have set the tone of the Buddhist area and its way of life.

To turn again to the analogy with the situation in the Western world, if taken in its scriptural form Christianity will be seen to be greatly different from the Christianity which is operative today in its Roman Catholic, Eastern Orthodox, and Protestant expressions. Yet each of these groups would claim that they are true to the basic teachings of early Christianity. In their adjustment to human life and problems in the world they have not given up the ideal view of man and his relationship to God upon which they ultimately rest. Yet, of necessity they have recognized that adjustments must be made between the ideal and the realm of the actual. And in all too many instances the ideal has been confused with the actual by the average Christian to the degree that they have been assumed to be nearly identical.

For Buddhism much the same is true. Buddhism is in conflict with the modern spirit in the degree that Christianity is in conflict with it. Christianity has made the adjustment to a larger degree, it is true, but Buddhism has made similar adjustments in the past and there is no reason why it should not make the adjustment now required of it. The problem is as to whether the fundamental view of Buddhism toward existence and salvation from the sufferings which existence in-

volves can maintain itself at all in the modern secular world
where life to the average man is becoming more and more
materially enriched.

B. BUDDHISM: THE INTERNAL TENSIONS

We have pointed to the extreme difficulty which faces one
when he seeks to discuss such complex phenomena as the
leading religions of the world. In the case of Buddhism it is
necessary to discuss what might be termed two separate religions, or possibly, many separate religions which are united
only on the most tenuous grounds. Through the course of its
history Buddhism has expressed itself in a multitude of forms,
each form intimately related in some fashion to the common
source of all Buddhism, and, yet, each form in one manner or
another adding more to the total Buddhist religious experience and body of thought. In the great majority of instances
the non-Buddhist investigator would be inclined to hold that
these additions, while possibly of value to the religious life of
the people, cannot properly be said to be in conformity with
the original emphases of the Faith.

Buddhism shares with Hinduism in the lack of an organizational consciousness in the degree that the Western religions
have conceived of themselves as bodies of believers united
around a common doctrine. Buddhism differs from Hinduism
in that it does possess a monastic conception (Sangha) which
it has inherited from the earliest days of its existence. However, the order of monks or professional full-time religious
devotees has always been limited to those who are prepared
to follow the religious life fully and completely. The only
exceptions to this are in the few areas such as Thailand where
the nation itself has sometimes been called a nation of monks.
Otherwise, there has existed a separation between the organized or formalized expression of Buddhism and the average citizen of the area which has meant that there has been
only a general consciousness of belonging to Buddhism. In
most Buddhist groups there has not been a definite act of
commitment in which the individual layman has been aware

that he was entering into a specific fellowship and proclaiming that he holds certain things to be true.

Among those who do give themselves to the religious life there has been, by and large, little consciousness of their relationship and duty to the laity. They have existed apart from the people as far as their religious interests are concerned, immersed in contemplative theological speculation in their best moments, or giving themselves to forms of monastic indolence in their worst moments. In any case, they have not contributed generally to a vital active religious consciousness on the part of all people in Buddhist lands which has resulted in the majority of the members of Buddhist society being alive to the demands of their religious faith and prepared to give themselves in whole-hearted support to its program. In fact, from the Western point of view a program of action has been missing in Buddhism except in the case of certain denominational or sectarian groups within northern Buddhism. This lack of organization and of a program of activity which includes the whole of Buddhist society is a primary weakness of Buddhism in the present situation which confronts it.

A more obvious, and more simply defined, weakness lies in the conflict of Buddhism with itself due to the broad divisions which separate it theologically and geographically; in this it shares with Christianity. Southern Pali or Theravadin Buddhism, commonly called Hinayana in the West, has ideally sought to preserve the original emphases of the teachings of the Buddha; Northern Buddhism, commonly called Mahayana, has flowered into a multiformed theological system including within itself almost every possible theological expression, though it has maintained that it is true to the highest teachings of the Buddha. In each case the objective non-Buddhist investigator is doubtful of the claims of either to being in any real sense pure expositions of original Buddhism. However, their claims and counterclaims in this regard are a source of constant conflict within the religion as a whole. Despite a consciousness of unity which centers around the person of the

Buddha on the part of the more intellectual Buddhists of both groups, Buddhists of one group on the whole are little conscious of a living fellowship with their fellow Buddhists in the other group. The lack of organizations and programs has contributed to this separation in that there have been few real attempts to overcome this religious provincialism.

This lack of organizational unity on a broad scale is to be found in both of the major divisions. In Theravadin Buddhism individual monasteries exist to themselves as separate entities with little or no real consciousness of a great unity which could enlist their separate energies. It is only in the last years that loose associations or co-operative enterprises have drawn them together, and in this they have followed the pattern of the modern spirit of corporate activity. Southern Buddhism is pre-eminently a monasticism and, despite claims to the contrary, has left the religious yearnings of the people to be filled by other religious forces—forces which are often primitive in character.

Mahayana Buddhism in the North has demonstrated a much greater organizing capacity, but this has contributed to disunity rather than unity. The situation in Northern Buddhism may be compared in many ways to the denominational sectarian condition of Protestant Christianity. These denominations or sects have arisen in some cases from the specific theological position of a school of Buddhist thinkers, in some instances they are based primarily upon a particular Buddhist scripture, and in others they are the result of the teaching and organizational ability of a single religious leader. Northern Buddhism in general has been more sensitive to the religious needs and hopes of the people as a whole and as a result has expressed itself in methods which have brought it closer to the people. The problem at the present time for Mahayana Buddhism is to what extent it can bring these separate expressions of Buddhist religious insight into a co-operating fellowship whereby unity, despite theological diversity, is the rule rather than disunity and weakness because of different interpretations of a common body of thought.

C. BUDDHISM : THE VARIETY OF THOUGHT

Something of the nature of the theological conflict within Buddhism has been indicated by our previous discussion. The underlying issue which separates Northern and Southern Buddhism is a theological one. It is of such magnitude that it has resulted for all practical purposes in the creation of two separate religions; indeed, more technical discussions of the world's religions often treat them as such. The geographic separation which is also involved has meant that the theological difference has not been in the nature of a conflict until in the last decades during which physical distances have ceased to be the factor they once were.

Southern Buddhism is essentially and theoretically a religious system which places its emphasis upon individual attainment of salvation. Holding that the experience of enlightenment which was realized by the Buddha is attainable by other human individuals who will follow his path, it has held up the monastic life as the ideal means whereby individuals might follow in his footsteps. Living the religious life of the monk, and separating himself from concerns with the mundane world, the individual has before him the possibility of becoming an Arhant, an enlightened one who no longer is tied to the world of existence, but who has now entered into Nibbana or the state beyond existence where the pains, sufferings, and struggles of the world do not exist. The individual layman of the Faith has a place in this only in that he is to follow the rules for the layman, rules which gradually will prepare him for such an undertaking in some future earthly existence.

Northern Buddhism is the exponent of a means of salvation whereby individual man is not ultimately dependent upon himself for salvation, but, rather, is the recipient of the love and concern of others who have attained, or are at the verge of attaining, release from existence. In place of the Arhant of the Southern school, Mahayana Buddhism has the Bodhisattva, the individual who through the process of many earthly and supra-earthly existences has come to the point where he may enter into "non-existence," but who out of concern and love for mankind remains in a dimension where he may serve men as their savior. The Bodhisattva thus becomes the object of devotion of the mass of the people; he is the recipient of prayers, the solace in trouble, the guide in action and, above all, the bestower of hope. Mahayana Buddhism, therefore, replaces the non-theism of theoretical Theravadin Buddhism with a personal theism which gives the individual layman a consciousness of the Divine or supra-human.

It will be noticed that it has been necessary to speak of "theoretical" Southern Buddhism. It would also be correct to do so in the case of Northern Buddhism. This is true in the first instance because the layman of the South has not been content to live in the atheistic view of existence which Theravadin thought has held. In the second instance it is true in that Mahayana on its highest intellectual levels has continued to maintain a metaphysics which denies the existence of a creator deity or a philosophical absolute; however, this also has not been closely associated with the religious thought of the laity.

This differentiation between the theological theory of the two branches of Buddhism and the religious thought and practice of the masses points to a conflict within Buddhism which it shares with the other major religions of the world. In its process of expansion over the greater part of Eastern Asia, Buddhism drew into itself the religious beliefs and cultic practices of the native peoples. In so doing it did not demand the outright cessation of these beliefs and customs but, rather, it gave them a place in its own system. Therefore, the Buddhism of today is not only a highly refined system of philosophical and psychological thought; in both of its major divisions it is a varied mass of beliefs and practices reflecting all levels of religious expression.

Therefore, while it is possible for certain Buddhist thinkers to say with at least some justification that Buddhism is in accord with the materialistic conception of the universe which is commonly associated with the scientific mind, yet it must be recognized that they are speaking for a refined and intellectual level which does not at all reflect the popular Buddhism of the masses. Buddhism is in conflict with itself on this point in the same degree as the other religions of the world. And because it has allowed the unintellectual expressions of the mass mind to exist without any noticeable protest on its part and has, indeed, encouraged such beliefs, it finds itself today in the position where it cannot legitimately declare itself independent of them without cutting itself off from the millions which are its supporters.

III. THE CONFLICT BETWEEN RELIGIONS: RELIGIOUS KNOWLEDGE AND THE DIVINE

The preceding discussions of the four dominant religions of the world have served to make clear that each of the religions is involved to some extent in a conflict with the general spirit and temper of the present epoch of history. They are also separately engaged in factional struggles within themselves which contribute to a situation of disunity both in their organizational structure and theological thought. The fact that it is possible to establish the existence of such conflict without penetrating in an exhaustive fashion into the more technical aspects of the religion indicates quite obviously that we are confronted today by a world religious situation wherein none of the leading religions of the world can be assumed to be secure in the decades immediately ahead.

It is not the conviction of the writer that religion as it is now conceived is in its last moments of history. On the contrary, even a cursory glance at religion throughout the world would seem to indicate the opposite to be true. The ability of religion around the world to hold the allegiance of millions of diverse peoples; the dynamic approach of various groups within the world religions to the problems of the day; the degree to which the major religions are now engaging in penetrating self-criticism; the extent to which religion in its different forms participates in the daily life of humanity; the intensity in which the religions are now engaged in cultivation and expansionist activities—these cannot be dismissed in any attempt to assess the contemporary world scene. Despite the lethargy, stultifying conservatism, and weaknesses to be found in each of the religions, in some form of expression and to some degree they share in this vitality.

We are now concerned to come to an understanding of the conflicts between the leading religions in the sphere of their theoretical, or theological, presuppositions. The conflicts of the various world religions with each other arise ultimately from their differences in theory. That is to say, a religion is based upon a theory of the nature of existence; it arises from a fundamental conception as to the meaning of Being. All of that which falls into man's consciousness is somehow arranged, classified, identified, accepted, rejected, understood, within the theoretical presuppositions of each major religion. Life is made understandable to the adherent of a religion because that religion has at its roots conceptions which determine the world view of all who participate in the Faith.

The use of the word "theoretical" in reference to the theological presuppositions of a religion is helpful in that it underlines that theology is constructed upon presuppositions which are in the nature of "theory." Theology in any of the major religions is not erected upon verifiable "fact" which can be established by objective investigation in the world of empirical reality. For that matter, it would be difficult to find any area of human concern where one could say this is "fact" and that is "theory." The discovery of a "fact," and its acceptance as a "fact," both rest upon belief as to how a "fact" is to be ascertained and on what grounds it is to be incorporated into human thought. Most important of all, "fact," "isness," or "verifiability" are concepts which ultimately rest upon the presupposition that such categories are of the nature of that which man can establish, and that the realities expressed by the concepts exist or are perceptible in the spheres of Time and Space in which man participates.

It is important, therefore, that the theoretical presuppositions underlying each religion and its theology be held up to view. The assumptions upon which a religion rests are the clue to the nature of the religion and the direction its thought and activity will take. They are theoretical in that they lie beyond the realm of rational or physical proof, and can be considered as established or verified only by those who accept them as more than theory by an act of faith.

It must be borne in mind that for the individual within the religious system the foundations upon which the system rests are not conceived as being "theoretical"; they are not presuppositions for the purpose of speculation. On the contrary, these basic tenets are Truth, Eternal Absolute Truth! For the Muslim or the Christian it is inconceivable that Allah or God is simply a presupposition upon which to erect a theory of the nature of existence and man's place in it. For the Hindu or the Buddhist it is not a matter of theory that life at any one moment is conditioned by acts in previous lives; this is not merely a convenient method of explaining or justifying the present condition of man. These matters which are approached as "theory" by the observer require that they be appreciated as constituting "certainties" for the adherent to the particular religious faith.

A religious certainty is that which is an intellectual theory or theological presupposition transposed into the sphere of the daily living of the Faith where it is held to be an Eternal Truth. From the perspective of the participant it gives cohesion and intelligibility to existence; from the approach of an observer it is a constituent part of a speculative system which is to be judged on rational grounds and in terms of human values. For the one, Truth is given and is participated in; for the other, Truth is to be established and only then is it to be considered worthy of acceptance as meaningful and demanding.

We shall endeavor in the following pages to indicate certain major areas of theological thought where the religions we have been discussing are in conflict with each other. It is obvious, of course, that in certain matters they are in agreement, if not in precise statement, at least in spirit. However, for the moment it is our task to discern the divisive factors which must be recognized by all those who look to religion for guidance in the meeting of the problems of the present age.

The theoretical basis of a religion has been said to express itself in three forms: the theory as to the nature of the Divine, the theory as to the nature of man, and the theory as to the nature of the world. A religion expresses its theoretical presuppositions most clearly in what it has to say concerning these three areas of human concern and speculation. God, man, the world or universe—these are the foundation stones of human wondering and the eternal search for meaning. The nature of that which is the source of what man experiences; the constitution, reason for being and ultimate destiny of that which experiences; the nature, processes, and relation of that which is experienced to the ultimate source of existence—these are the areas of the theoretical expression, the theological construction of a religion. With them as a base many and varied systems are erected. Each system has its own particular set of theories concerning the individual problems, each has its own method of approach and separate conclusions. This is true whether we are speaking of separate systems of religions or of different systems within one religion. However, amidst the variety similarity and sometimes an elementary uniformity is discernible. Where the ultimate concerns are of a like nature it is not unexpected that similar questions and like answers will sometimes occur.

For our purposes we shall deal with these fundamental theoretical concerns of the religious mind of man in four areas in which the separate religions are vitally concerned today, and to which they have devoted some of their best minds durings their history—Religious Knowledge, the Divine, Man, and Human Fulfilment.

1. Religious Knowledge

The problem of epistemology is one which has intrigued thinkers throughout the history of human thought. Just how does man obtain knowledge? By what independent means can such knowledge be verified, and on what grounds can man establish that his verified knowledge is correlative with Absolute Truth? Further, on what basis can man hold or assume that there is such a thing or existent as Absolute Truth? Are there evidences verifiable in the human dimension which establish the existence of that which is True, Absolute, Eternal, and subject to nothing outside Itself? Such questions have involved the whole of the history of philosophy and, obviously, are beyond our scope in this discussion. But, they point to something which lies at the heart of today's conflict of thought —the acceptance or rejection by men of the conception of the existence of that which is Eternal and Absolute in the midst of, or outside of, that which is momentary and dependent.

For religion this involved problem is as fundamental as it is for any philosophy. In the religious realm it revolves around the problem of *Religious Knowledge*. How does man gain any knowledge, any concepts, any insights into the nature of Truth, and are the beliefs he holds verifiable? More precisely, the question ultimately is concerned with whether or not the religious beliefs of man are subjective and, therefore, shaped by individual limitations and fancies, or whether they are founded on a source which Itself is Truth. In other words, from where does religious belief come, and on what grounds may it be held to be authoritative?

A. THE CHRISTIAN PRESUPPOSITION

Christianity has been involved in this question since its earliest history and, in the main, has held to a position which is in accord with its Semitic origins. The position can be stated as follows: There is one God who created all that physically exists, who is concerned with the affairs and fate of man in the world, and who has in the past and does in the present make Himself known to man by various means. It will be observed at once that the foregoing is intimately related to the usual and accepted creedal statements of the Christian Church; and, also, it will be noticed that this position immediately implies certain conceptions concerning God, Man, and the World.

Religious knowledge, therefore, is derived by man from God either in a direct or indirect fashion. Orthodox Christianity has held that religious knowledge in any significant degree is the result of direct action by God, and in any degree whatsoever results from divine act and not human attainment. The most decisive instances of the giving of this knowledge to man by God are those recorded in the Old and New Testaments, and the greatest in content, quality, and importance is that to be found in the person and activities of Jesus of Nazareth. This greatest revelation, in fact, is seen from the Christian perspective as being so totally unlike all other revelation of religious knowledge that it must be said to be *the* unique and decisive point in human history. In this event God was not only acting, He was present, He became man. From that moment on man has had available to him religious knowledge which is richer than any insights possessed by men previously. And, most important of all, this religious knowledge is to be equated with Truth, and is Eternal Truth, because it has been conveyed to man by the Source of Truth, the God who is Truth.

Further, Christianity has held that a knowledge of religious Truth and insight into Truth is not dependent alone upon an event in the historic past, but it continually is made available to man by God's operation in the world through the Holy Spirit, which is God present now in the dimension of man. Thus, religious knowledge is brought to each successive generation of individuals, it is enriched and made meaningful at every stage of life, and it is made operative in every epoch of human history as the great event in which it was made available to man constantly is being renewed through the continued activity of God in the lives of men.

The foregoing general statement of an involved theological position succeeds only in conveying the broadest outline of the Christian conception of religious knowledge. A mere listing of the names of Christian theologians who have developed variations upon this theme would fill more than the page upon which this is written. Each of these variations, however, has been grounded upon the presuppositions which support the central theme.

This Christian theory or belief concerning revelation is centered in Jesus Christ. Christian orthodoxy has not wavered in its emphasis upon the part played by Christ in bringing to man *the* knowledge of God, of man's nature, and the place of man in the divine scheme of existence. Almost all forms of Christian heterodoxy also have held revelation to have been the act of Christ, and have not questioned the ultimate and true nature of the revelation. Without Christ man's perception of God was at best faulty and incomplete; with Christ and in him all things were made known to the eyes of faith.

The term "the eyes of faith" points to the central factor in much of the controversy over revelation which has taken place throughout Christian history. It is not enough to say that religious knowledge is the direct result of an act done by a supra-human being or agency. When this has been said, the problem remains as to what part is played in revelation by the recipient—man. Does he act as the clay upon which the revelation is written, passively receiving the imprint but nothing more? Obviously, he responds to the divine initiative made known in revelation, but by what means, and is the response really his or is it and its nature pre-determined by God? More specifically, is the response of man to the revelation of God in Jesus Christ a response of man's reason or of his emotions of fear and hope? We have entered here into a primary concern of Christian theology and of present-day religious psychology.

The problem of religious knowledge has become, therefore, a problem of the nature of man and his response to the divine act of revelation. While not ruling out the possibility of lesser degrees of revelation in other events and areas, and in some cases placing emphasis upon such revelation, Christianity ultimately rests upon the revelation of God and of Truth which it claims to be in the acts and person of Jesus Christ. This is given; it is beyond question; it is "fact." But, this body of revealed Truth must pass through the process of entering the human mind and winning the allegiance of man. Does Truth maintain its objective stature as it undergoes the process of becoming religious knowledge? To what degree is its objectivity replaced by the subjective and finite nature of the man who now has received it and is incorporating it into his own dimensions and limitations of thought? What is the place of human reason in this process, and what is the function of that which is called "faith"?

The Christian religion is confronted by a limited set of possibilities in its theory of religious knowledge. Having at its center the conviction of a divinely given body of such knowledge, it has the alternative to hold that this knowledge is perceptible to man through his inherent religious nature, through his rational faculties, or by the imposition of it upon man by a fiat of God. All three of these positions have been maintained by Christian thinkers. They have been held exclusively and inclusively, but in most instances in the last centuries emphasis has been given to the place of the inherent God-given religious nature of man and its response to the divine initiative of revelation and redemption.

Christianity has been in internal conflict over this question primarily in the matter of the place of human reason in the perception of religious knowledge. It is basic to Christianity that such knowledge is not the result of the probing, searching human mind; the knowledge itself is the direct result of God's act in history. However, the degree to which the human mind is capable of using the knowledge is another matter. Since such knowledge is Truth, is it to be subjected to the criticisms and investigations of the human reason? If some aspect of the Truth appears to be incongruous with the conclusions of human reason is it to be concluded without question that the error is on the part of the reason? Is human reason, therefore, to be limited by the structure of revealed Truth which is central to the Christian religion?

The question can also be raised as to whether or not the reason is involved in the determination of the content and meaning of the originally given religious knowledge. Setting aside the very important question as to the function of man in the recording and transmission of that knowledge, is there any point outside the act of revelation itself in which reason has not played a central part? Unless it is held that the proper interpretations of the given religious knowledge have been given only under direct fiat from God, there is no escape from the conclusion that religious knowledge possessed by the Christian Faith as a result of the gift of God has been and is subject to the abilities and limitations of the human reason.

It has been necessary to digress into the foregoing general discussion of the relation between revelation and reason (a subject to which some of the most learned works of Christian theology have been devoted) in order to indicate the relationship between Christianity and the contemporary scientific rational spirit of the day. Despite its emphasis upon religious knowledge in its finest sense being given to man by an act of God, Christianity in most of its expressions has given a large place to the application of human reason to the knowledge received from God. Therefore, theological construction and speculation has had a place in Christian activity. True, there have been restrictions placed upon that activity, but the process of bringing the reason to play upon the body of knowledge has resulted in a health and vitality which has often challenged the restrictions. There has been an oft-recurring tension between the position which holds the religious knowledge to be supra-rational and that which has insisted upon the necessity of the application of reason to the Truth revealed primarily in Christ, recorded in the Christian Scriptures, and witnessed to by the Christian Church.

The theory of religious knowledge held by Christianity and evidenced in the many writings on the problem throughout

Christian history is one which holds to two primary fundamentals. First, God has revealed Himself in one unique moment in human history as well as in other moments of less decisive character, and secondly, the revelation is meaningful to humanity through man's divinely given capacity for response—a response which involves among other things the function of human rationality though the content of the revelation may be supra-rational in its final essence.

B. THE MUSLIM PRESUPPOSITION

The theory of religious knowledge held by Islam is one which participates in many of the main features of that held by Christianity. There is one God, Allah, who is the creator of that which is, and who has revealed Himself in a series of revelations to man which culminated in the supreme revelation given through the agency of the man Muhammad, and recorded in the Koran. Again, there is evidenced a concrete presupposition as to the existence of one God who is in relationship with man and the world. We shall see that the nature of Allah, of man, and the relationship of Allah to the world is not identical with that held by Christianity, but at this juncture the point to be observed is that the Muslim conception of religious knowledge is, at its base, identical with that of Christianity. Allah is the initiator, the bestower of religious knowledge, and man is the recipient. This knowledge is Truth; it is Truth because it has been given by that which is both the Source of Truth and Truth Itself—Allah!

Very early in Muslim history the problem arose as to the relationship between revelation and reason. The totally other nature of Allah from that of man which was disclosed in the Koran made the outcome of the controversy obvious. Holding the Koran to be completely supra-human in nature and not the product of human effort, orthodox Islam ultimately resolved the problem by concluding that the revelation was absolutely superior to human reason and was not to be considered to be subject to the processes of rationality. The controversy was not settled without bitter struggles in which some of the greatest figures of Muslim history participated. On the surface certain concessions were made to the place of human reason, but fundamentally Islamic thought remained wedded to the belief that Islam was the possessor of Ultimate Truth revealed by the Divine and beyond all human questioning and criticism.

We have indicated in a previous discussion that the contemporary struggles of Islam with the spirit of the age have led a few modern Muslim thinkers to seek a new approach to the Koran. Their intense struggles with the conservative body of Islamic interpreters and thinkers are indicative of the degree to which the present orthodox view of the nature of the revelation in the Koran continues to be that of the past. Even in those instances where these modern scholars have maintained that there is no necessary disjunction between revelation and reason they have not always received the sympathetic support of the conservative scholars; for even in this they are qualifying the supra-human nature of the revelation.

The underlying presupposition of all of Muslim theology is that Allah has acted in giving religious knowledge to mankind in a supreme historical event. If an individual accepts this presupposition as an article of faith and removes it from the realm of theory, he has become a Muslim; if not, he is an unbeliever. For orthodox Islam the only method whereby an individual may participate in any degree in religious knowledge without being a Muslim is to be found in his allegiance to the prior revelations given by Allah before the supreme revelation disclosed to Muhammad. Such people, the "followers of the books," are represented today by the Jews, Christians, and Parsees of India. But, at best, they are in possession of religious knowledge which is highly limited and of little value when seen in the light of the supreme revelation contained in the Koran. By their refusal to accept this final revelation they have declared themselves to be opponents of Ultimate Truth—they have refused to "submit" to It.

It must be added that the Christian and Islamic conceptions of religious knowledge are not only those represented in the orthodox views which we have just indicated. Every religion has produced those groups which have not limited themselves to the accepted or orthodox position regarding religious knowledge. Such divisions within the religion may or may not accept the orthodox doctrine, but in either case they add to it by holding that there are other sources for the knowledge of Ultimate Truth. These groups, which are present in both Islam and Christianity, usually find such knowledge through the agency of the direct contact of the Divine with man. Such a contact may be in the form of an "Inner Light" or "Divine Spark" possessed by all men, or it may be considered to be limited to certain unique individuals who by one means or another possess a contact with the Divine which is not shared by all men.

We shall see this position in a larger context when we discuss Buddhism and Hinduism, but it would not be sufficient to assume that it has not had its place in the development of Muslim and of Christian theology. Both of these religions have within themselves groups which place emphasis upon such knowledge, though in many cases the orthodox body of the Faith is skeptical of, if not actively opposed to, such a concept of revelation. Where this knowledge is not in opposition or contradiction to the supreme revelation of the Faith it often has been hailed as evidence of the working of the Divine in the hearts of those who immerse themselves more deeply into the content of the revelation. But, whenever such religious knowledge has in any way challenged the majority conception of the supreme revelation, it has been considered heresy and not Truth.

In actual historic practice both Christianity and Islam have given a place to this added concept of religious knowledge. The Christian belief in the presence of the Holy Spirit will not allow Christianity to be totally disdainful of those individuals who claim to possess religious insights which go beyond those possessed by the majority of Christians. The Muslim theory of the direct intervention of Allah in the life and thought of man, and of His presence in the heart, will not allow Islam to rule out the real possibility of individuals expressing Truths which are not fully known by the body of Muslims. But, in either case such religious knowledge may not be in contradiction to the supreme revelation upon which the religion rests, and is accepted only as a further understanding of that which was previously divinely bestowed.

A study of the Eastern religions, Hinduism and Buddhism, reveals that the conceptions of religious knowledge upon which they rest are at the same time similar and dissimilar to those of Christianity and Islam. We are not dealing with simple, uncomplex areas of thought in which the fundamental presuppositions and their exposition are clearly in direct antithesis to each other. The religious experience of mankind is of like nature to such a degree that even obviously opposing systems participate in aspects common to all. A common humanity will not react to its religious yearnings and its encounter with the Divine in totally unlike ways. We are seeking to come to an understanding of the varied and conflicting nature of the world's leading religions, but in doing this, we must not overlook the universal elements present in all manifestations of religion.

C. THE HINDU PRESUPPOSITION

Hinduism is not the result of the work of a personal founder who gave to the religion a definite core of presuppositions which can be found in a body of scripture. It does not express itself in and through a clearly defined institution which considers itself to be the guardian of such presuppositions. The presuppositions which are basic to Hinduism are incorporated into a body of writings and accepted as the "Truth" concerning the nature of existence not because they are held to be the *one* self-revelation of the Divine, but because they are the result of a series of divine revelations and human perceptions of those revealed truths. The very nature of Hinduism is such that revelation is conceived in a different sense than that which we have observed in the previous religions.

It is said that the majority of Hindus are united in the

belief in the divine origin of the early Vedic writings of the period of the Aryan invasions into India. This is true only if it is said in the broadest sense possible. It is true that conservative Hinduism looks to the Vedas as being *sruti,* or divinely given. However, whereas one could say that the majority of Christians and Muslims have some knowledge of their sacred scriptures, at least that they consider them to be sacred and are aware of their central basic place in the religion, it would be difficult to establish that such would be true in the case of Hindus. The educated or religiously alert Hindu knows something of the Vedas, he can quote from them, but he does not find in them the religious value that the average Christian or Muslim would claim to find in the Bible or the Koran. Further, and most important, the Hindu finds his greatest source of religious Truth in great theological-philosophical works which are later than the Vedic period; he finds his religious inspiration in devotional literature which is not identified in a specific fashion with the Vedas.

However, it is correct to consider the Vedas as revelation if we do not carry over the general Western connotations of the word. Holding the Vedas to be the products of the great Rishis or religious "seers" of antiquity, the Hindu considers them to be sacred in character. This sacredness is due to the fact that the Vedas were given by the Divine (Brahman) to the Rishis. The Rishis "saw" them, that is they came to know the Truths which Brahman gave or placed within their reach. Brahman did not act in one great decisive moment when Eternal Truth was brought into the finite realm of man. Rather, Brahman made Himself available to those men who were worthy and prepared for the Truth, and these in turn passed the Truth on to those after them who would be worthy.

Orthodox Hinduism is committed in this way to the theory of divine acts of self-revelation whereby Truth is made available to man. The point of difference from the beliefs of the Western religions is that this is not held to be one act which is final and in any sense complete, nor is it the culmination of a series of acts which have preceded it. There does not seem to be, at least in the case of the Vedas, the conception that this revelation is done purely out of the concern of the Divine for contact with man in which He will establish His will or reveal His nature. The Divine merely makes Truth available to those who desire it enough to be prepared to receive it, and who by their preparations have made themselves worthy to "see" it.

The Vedas generally are held by most Hindus to contain within themselves all necessary Truth whereby man can discover the correct knowledge as to his situation and destiny. In this sense the Vedas are the containers of divinely given Truth. But, again, it must be realized that this Truth is that which has been seen by the saints of old because of the act of the Divine. The Divine is basic to the whole conception of religious knowledge, but man and his perception of this Truth is equally necessary.

The Upanishads, that great body of theological-philosophical literature which contains the essence of Hindu thought, are considered by Hindus to be further explications of the Truth found in the Vedas. These are not divinely given in the same sense as are the Vedas, yet they contain the Truth which is in the Vedas in that they are human reflections upon that Truth. They are Vedanta, the end or summation of that which is in the Vedas. Throughout Hindu history, since their origin around the sixth century B.C., they have stood as the prime source for Hindu religious and philosophical thought. The Hindu thinker today who wishes to quote authority for a belief will often turn to them for support rather than to the Vedas.

It is at this point that the difference between Hindu and Western religious conceptions of religious knowledge becomes most clear. For the Hindu the primary source of knowledge concerning Truth is not to be found in a divinely given body of thought preserved in writing; it is to be obtained from the insights of those who by their own efforts have come to understand the Truth which the Divine has given to them. For Hinduism human effort takes on a much more significant role than it does for either Christianity or Islam. It is in human effort that Truth is obtained and not by a specific act of the Divine.

It is difficult to be precise at this point because care must be made that the impression is not given that the Divine does not act. All too many Western interpreters of Hinduism have assumed that the Divine, for Hinduism, is a far-removed Being unmindful of man and his situation. The Upanishads make it clear, however, that the Divine only reveals Himself to those to whom He desires. There is a divine act, or more precisely, a series of divine acts in which Brahman reveals Himself to man. Any system of belief which posits the existence of a divine Being upon whom human material existence in some way depends must place the divine act of revelation prior to the apprehension of the Divine by finite man. For orthodox Hinduism, however, the revelation as it is known by man is the result of human probings into the Truth, and not so much simply divine giving of the Truth.

The divine revelation is not limited to the Vedas alone. There have been other acts of revelation which have been preserved for man within the structure of Hinduism. These revelations are the products of two activities or sources which we shall see in our discussion of the nature of man to be ultimately one and the same source in many forms of Hindu thought. These sources are the Divine and the human. The Divine is not absent from the human temporal sphere except, perhaps, for the most refined Hindu metaphysical thought, and there it is present in a different manner. The Divine is constantly appearing in human history guiding men and making Itself and Truth known to man. A large body of Hindu religion is gathered around the conception of the Divine becoming incarnate in the form of *avataras* or God in human form teaching man. These avataras or incarnations in many cases are the most revered deities in the Hindu pantheon. They are the heroes of the great myths and epics, and are the deities to whom man looks in his desire for supra-human comfort and companionship. The two great Hindu epics, the Mahabharata and the Ramayana, are the stories of two of the primary avataras who were the Divine on earth aiding man.

Again, the Divine is known to man by the female deities—the consorts of the great gods who represent the divine power. Religious knowledge comes from them in that they are constantly available to humanity revealing the compassion, the anger, the concern of the Divine for even the petty things of human existence. On the lower mass levels of Hinduism these great female deities are followed by scores of lesser deities who are close to man and to whom man turns in his worship. The sense of the Divine given by these lesser forms of divinity conveys to man a consciousness of the Divine which must be considered religious knowledge. Though it is not of the refined nature of the Upanishads and their theological-philosophical speculation, this religious knowledge does convey the awareness of the nearness of divinity which is present in the Vedas and in the great epic and devotional literature of Hinduism.

Another primary source for religious knowledge and one which is extremely important in the general structure of Hinduism is that of the religious genius—the saint, the theological speculator, the teacher of Truth, the *guru*—who has come to know the Truth by his own application to the Truth which the Divine is constantly revealing to those who seek. This is the human element in the revelation of the Divine, and for Hinduism it has been a fundamental means for the preservation of Truth and the attainment of it by succeeding generations. The path to religious knowledge may depend upon one's own abilities and the attainment of it upon the efforts of the individual, but each seeker does best by turning to those who have preceded him for guidance in his own endeavors. At the feet of his guru, or teacher, he begins his search guided by the insights of the saint who is further advanced than he. The guru expounds on the Truths which are preserved in the sacred writings and the speculations of the great religious men of the past, but more important, he instructs by example more than by words.

In the example which the holy men—the gurus, the *sanyasi*

—put before their student followers, something of the Divine Itself is to be seen. Man himself reveals the Divine. Religious knowledge is not exclusively dependent upon an act of revelation, it is present in man himself. To anticipate our discussion of the Hindu presupposition concerning the nature of man, the Divine is in man to the degree that ultimate religious knowledge need not be sought in what is usually meant by revelation—a holy book, an incarnation of God, or a holy man—it is to be known through the efforts of the individual to know the true nature of himself.

Ultimately, then, in Hinduism religious knowledge is obtainable by the efforts of humanity to fathom the meaning of human existence. It is when man primarily by his own efforts, and with the help of the various divine means of guidance, has come to know himself and existence that man may be said to possess or know the Truth. In a later context we shall have occasion to discuss the means whereby man can attain to this knowledge, but at this point it must be made clear that Hinduism places its emphasis upon the attainment by man. The primary reason for the existence of Hinduism as a religion is to give to man the means whereby this knowledge can be attained. It is man's efforts, his following of the path of works, his dedication to the path of love, or his plunging into the way of mystical insight and intuition which is the central concern of Hindu teaching. We are not overlooking the existence in Hinduism of forms of religion which expect little of man, for even here good works or love toward the deity on the part of man are necessary and fundamental. Religious knowledge and salvation are eventually one and the same for Hinduism, and in each case they rest primarily upon man even though the Divine may initiate the action.

Broadly speaking, Hinduism has not had to face the question as to the relation between revelation and reason in the same manner as have the religions of the West. This is not so much due to a greater appreciation of the human reason as it is the result of the Hindu conception as to the means whereby religious knowledge is obtained. Though it appears to the outsider that Truth is gained in a large degree by the application of human speculation to the problems which confront man in his search for ultimate meaning, yet the great figures of Hinduism have not placed their emphasis upon thought in the normal sense of the word. Knowledge, as we have been speaking of it, is the result of what might more properly be called intuition, or better, by the meeting of the soul of man with the Soul of the Divine. In this meeting rationality is not a factor which decides the issue as to whether man apprehends the Truth confronting him. The issue is decided in the sudden intuitive insight wherein the individual man loses his consciousness of individuality and recognizes his relationship with Truth, or as we shall discover later, apprehends his own identity with Truth.

The line dividing reason and logical thought from intuition and non-rational apprehension is difficult to establish without appearing to appeal to something which is irrational and, in the minds of many, superstitious. The rational spirit of today is in a large measure the product of the Greek heritage of the West and is not content to accept the dictum that religious knowledge ultimately is beyond the confines of logical rational application. However, all of the religions finally make a retreat to the sphere of supra-rationality. They share in the conviction that the Truth which they proclaim and which is their reason for being in the last analysis is of a nature which lifts it beyond the limitations of the finite human mind. Of course, this is not to say that reason does not have its place within the human sphere of religious apprehension, for all the religions appeal to reason in some form and at some level, but in their orthodox forms they have not made their conceptions of religious knowledge coterminous with man's rational faculty.

D. THE BUDDHIST PRESUPPOSITION

Buddhism shares in a large measure in the view toward religious knowledge which we have ascribed to Hinduism. It is a product of the Hindu religious ethos and it has continued throughout its history to share with Hinduism in many of its basic presuppositions. However, Buddhism differs from Hinduism because it is the result of the religious experience of an historic individual. That individual, his teachings and his presuppositions, have given a mark to Buddhism which despite much straying from his original precepts has continued in one form or another down to the present. It is in him that Buddhism finds its fundamental source for religious knowledge.

Gautama, the Buddha, is looked to by all Buddhists as the pioneer of the way to salvation. It is in his experience of Enlightenment, *Bodhi*, that Buddhism has its beginnings. From his own experience the Buddha constructed the original system which set out to be the universal religion for mankind. He was both the discoverer and the revealer of the Truth of religious knowledge which will set men free from existence as they know it in the sphere of Time and Space.

Buddha serves a two-fold purpose in regard to religious knowledge. In the first place, he brings religious knowledge to mankind by sharing with men the Truth which he himself has discovered or experienced. While it was basic to his thought that to obtain the knowledge of Truth is to remove oneself from the human finite dimension, yet in his case he returned from that which is beyond humanity to instruct man in the path by which it can be reached. He is the revealer of religious knowledge in that he shows men the method by which it may be found. The Middle Path of religious realization is in itself religious knowledge of the highest sort since it is Truth as well as the means whereby Truth is to be obtained. The method of reaching the goal is of such a character that it participates in the nature of the goal itself; the means and the aim or end cannot be separated, for the end determines and, therefore, is an inherent part of the method to be employed.

Secondly, the Buddha did not confine himself to teaching the way to Enlightenment. The presupposition upon which he erected his whole system, the Four Fold Truth as to the nature of human existence and the means of escape from its sorrow, was the result of his own experience and of his Enlightenment; it obviously was not in contradiction to his highest insight. From this it can be seen that the Buddha himself was the source of knowledge of the Truth. Each presupposition upon which he erected his system is held by Buddhists to be the result of his act of attaining to Truth and participating in it. The nature of man and the human situation; the method by which man may rise above that situation; the state of man beyond the present existence—all of these are Truth and are revealed by the Buddha himself.

Thus, Buddhism has at its core a source for religious knowledge to which it looks for its fundamental beliefs, and upon which it attempts to build its various systems. Yet, Buddhism shares with Hinduism in its conviction that religious knowledge ultimately is obtained by the individual himself as a result of his own application and effort toward realizing it. Religious knowledge in the finite realm is the result of the Enlightenment of the Buddha and of his sharing with men those aspects of his experience which can be expressed in human terms. However, religious knowledge in its more precise and ultimate sense is the goal of Buddhism rather than its content. It is only when the individual has himself experienced Enlightenment that he may properly be said to *know* the Truth; only then is Truth in its fulness united to man. But, in the moment of Enlightenment finite man ceases to be finite. He has risen above the limitations of human existence and now participates in religious knowledge in its totality. The teachings of the Buddha are filled with religious knowledge and, therefore, are Truth; but they are preparatory to a final and full religious knowledge wherein the possession of Truth by the seeker means escape from the world, or salvation.

Southern Theravadin Buddhism is rather easily identified with the belief concerning religious knowledge which we have just outlined. Its ideal continues to be the following of the precepts of the Buddha as they are revealed in the Pali

scriptures, the Tipitika, which supposedly contain the core
of the Buddha's teaching. The scriptures themselves, of course,
are sources for knowledge of the Truth since they are the
written record of the Buddha's precepts. The person who
enters the religious life and sets out on the search for Truth
has at his disposal the necessary aid of the Tipitika. He is
also dependent upon the knowledge he can gain, both written
and oral, from the seekers of the past and the masters of the
present. Each successive seeker after Truth puts himself in
the path taken by others before him; joining with them in
devotion to the path revealed by the Buddha; participating in
the community of seekers founded by the Buddha; and placing his trust in the pioneer who blazed the path which he follows, the Buddha himself.

Northern Mahayana Buddhism in the main has no disagreement with what has been said, but one of its chief characteristics is that it has added further sources of religious
knowledge to those already mentioned. In a later discussion
of basic Buddhist presuppositions we shall discover that the
Buddha is held to be of a different nature than orthodox
Southern Buddhism would allow. Northern Buddhism believes that the revelation of Truth which was given by the
Buddha is not confined to those Pali scriptures which are
recognized by Southern Buddhism. In his latter days the
Buddha revealed a stage of Truth greater than that which he
originally gave to his followers. At first they were only spiritually mature enough to receive the lower stage of Truth, but
before he left them he gave to them an added insight which is
the highest which finite man is capable of receiving.

This higher stage or level of Truth is contained in a group
of scriptures which contain the fundamental religious beliefs
of Mahayana Buddhism. Different denominations or sects of
Mahayana place varying degrees of emphasis upon these
scriptures, and some of them maintain that their particular
scripture contains in itself all religious knowledge and Truth
which in any way can be expressed in finite terms. Where
Theravadin Buddhism has tended to be a "scriptural" reli-

gion in its emphasis upon the Tipitika, Mahayana Buddhism in many of its expressions has definitely become "scriptural," holding these particular writings to be *the* source of religious knowledge.

It remains to be said that for Mahayana Buddhism, as with Theravadin Buddhism and Hinduism, Truth in its ultimate sense is identical with salvation, or release, from human existence. Therefore, here also religious knowledge is the fruit of application on man's part. It is by human effort and the following of the path of the Buddha that man finally attains to the supra-human sphere in which he and Truth are one. Northern Buddhism and Hinduism have a place for the gracious saving power of the Divine wherein it is not human effort but divine grace which gives man a place in a future heaven, and it is not totally absent from popular Southern Buddhism, but for neither is such a state of heavenly bliss the attainment of the final and total Truth which is ultimately dependent upon human effort no matter what amount of supra-human aid is available. Salvation, or future reward in a state after earthly life, in this instance is not coterminous with attainment of religious knowledge. For both of the great Eastern religions ultimate and final religious knowledge is identified with the highest form of salvation—the state of existence or being which is of a dimension totally unlike that known by man in his present state and, therefore, beyond earthly categories of description. To be in possession of religious knowledge in this sense is to have surmounted the limiting ties and shackles of earth-bound existence and to have attained Divinity. Religious Knowledge and God or Truth are one, and to possess the former is to be at one with the latter!

2. The Divine

It generally has been held that the essential characteristic of a religion is the belief in the existence of *the Divine*. The usual text book definitions of religion often make some reference to a God or a group of gods. Religion, it is usually believed, is primarily concerned with the relationship between humanity and divinity. It is true that with few exceptions the history of religion throughout the world is the history of man's beliefs and convictions concerning a power or powers outside himself which he has considered to be supra-human and either of a divine or demonic character. In many expressions of religious experience the dividing line between the divine and demonic is so fine that the demonic must also be said to be deity. The Divine is not limited to that which works only for man's welfare; it may be opposed to man, setting itself over against him in such a fashion that it is man's enemy. But even as foe, the divine element which confronts man is a primary concern of the religious systems which man creates. It is the Divine in all of Its manifestations with which we are now concerned as a primary presupposition of the major religions which we are discussing.

However, care must be taken that we do not insist upon a belief in the existence of the Divine as being a necessary part of a religion. The standard definitions of religion which have insisted upon a belief in deity as being essential to a religion would remove Theravadin Buddhism in its intellectual form from the religious category. Definitions of this type also fail to recognize that a belief in the Divine is but one part of a total whole which constitutes religion, and in some of the religions of the world it is not necessarily the primary concern of the religion. With the exception of Theravadin Buddhism a belief in the Divine is the foundation upon which the religious systems of mankind rest, but as they develop, religions may tend to accept this as a given fact and turn their attention more to the problem of man's salvation or to his ethical behavior.

Nevertheless, the reasons for ethical behavior and the possibility of some type of salvation for man in which he will find himself in a higher state of existence than what he now experiences, rest upon a presupposition of the existence of a divine element within the universe or cosmos. In the great majority of its forms religion does not recognize a purely utilitarian

ethic no matter how beneficial it may be; goodness and truth
are related to the nature of the Divine. It does not see the possibility of human salvation without the existence of an agency
which creates the potentiality; the fulfilment of man is related
to the Divine which is the source of man and all that is. Even
in Southern Buddhism this may be said to be true, for the religion of the masses of the people, to a large extent, has turned
its back upon the intellectual insistence upon a materialistic
world without a divine source.

A. THE CHRISTIAN VIEW

The Christian presupposition concerning the Divine is a
direct inheritance from Hebrew thought. Through the centuries of its development Hebrew religion had come to conceive
of God as a single spiritual Being who is in control of the
world and universe. For the Hebrew, God was personal in that
He is a unitary Being who enters into relationships with men
as a Person. He is not simply an essence that pervades existence. God was apprehended as a Being with purpose and will,
and that purpose and will were the direct result of God's nature. The revelation of God given to the Patriarchs, to Moses
at Mount Sinai, and to the prophets was one which revealed
a God unique in holiness and goodness. In the centuries of
progressive insight into the nature of God, the Hebrew people came to believe Him to be possessed of the highest moral
attributes. God and morality were more and more conceived
as being identical. It has not been without just cause that the
Hebraic-Jewish religion has been termed an "ethical monotheism." From the period of the great eighth-century B.C.
prophets on, the moral nature of God has been a central and
decisive factor shaping the whole of the religion.

In close relationship with the ethical monotheism which was
its most important possession, Hebraism held God to be
transcendent in nature and not identifiable with the world or
material existence. The world is dependent upon the Divine
both for its origin and for its maintenance; the Divine is not
dependent upon the world nor coterminous with it. However,

this transcendent God is also immanent. The Divine is near to man and is concerned with the affairs of man. He has revealed Himself to man in order that man may know of Him and His will. He is concerned that men fulfil His will for them, and in following God's commands men will gain IIis favor. Despite the transcendent nature of God, He has placed Himself in a covenantal relationship with men whereby He is vitally concerned in the affairs of this world, and serves as protector, law-giver, and judge. Nor has His transcendence kept Him from drawing near to men in intimate communion, and in this communion men may come to know the Divine as companion, comforter, and friend.

The close relationship between God and man exists on both the social and personal levels. In common with most early forms of religion, Hebraism first conceived of the relationship between God and man to be between God and man in community. It was the Hebrew community which was in a compact or covenant with God. This implies community responsibility to the Divine, and since the Divine is conceived as being righteous and demanding righteousness of His chosen community of men, that society must seek the righteousness that is the will of the Divine. With the development of a conception of personal responsibility and relationship to God, Hebraism came to hold that the covenant between God and man was also one between persons, the Divine Person and the individual human person. Here, too, ethical responsibility is central. It is not enough that the individual man recognizes or worships the Divine; he must also seek to implement the will of God through his own actions. Man is a responsible being and his responsibility is the result of the righteous ethical nature of God. The Divine, therefore, is a challenger to higher levels of moral living both to society and to individual men. Not only is He a comforter to His people, but He is a judge of their actions as well.

The Christian belief concerning the nature of the Divine incorporated all of the foregoing. Jesus was a Jew both by birth and by religious belief. The band of disciples and the early Christian community were composed of individuals who also participated in the Jewish heritage. They accepted the Jewish presuppositions concerning the nature of God and made it the foundation-stone of their own religious faith. Despite the fact that Greek thought concerning the Divine also played a part in the developing theoretical statements about God's nature, the core of Christian thought remained wedded to the ethical monotheism of Judaism.

Jewish scholars have insisted that Jesus added nothing new to the Jewish understanding of the nature of God. If it is meant that everything he said about God's nature and relationship to man can be found in some form in the Old Testament and Hebraic-Jewish thought, they are probably correct. However, there can be no doubt but that he went beyond Jewish thought in the depth of perception in which he understood the close relationship between God and man. In his awareness of the moral nature of the Divine, the love of God for even the evil man, the participation of God in the sorrows of individuals, the moral indignation of God at the evil actions of perverse mankind, the demand of God that men live and think righteously, and the forgiving nature of God toward those who are sincerely penitent—in these convictions concerning the Divine, Jesus combined all of the religious insights of the Psalmists, Prophets, and religious geniuses of the Hebraic-Jewish tradition in a manner which confronted men with an understanding of God which they had not gained in a comparable degree from Judaism itself.

Yet, even in all of the foregoing we have not touched directly upon the central presuppositions concerning God's nature which is the foundation upon which Christianity rests. The teaching of Jesus concerning God went beyond that already believed by the Jews primarily in his conviction of the relationship between himself and God. Jesus referred to God as Father, and by this he not only meant to be repeating a term which had been used before concerning God, but he was making clear that he himself participated in a unique manner in the divinity of God. Jesus was related to God as the Son; a relationship so close that he and his Father were and are one.

Early Christian theology was confronted by this identification of Jesus and God with a problem which has never been fully understood or accepted by those who are outside the Faith. In the days of early Christianity such thought was not foreign to mankind in the degree that it is today for many non-religious and religious people. The Greco-Roman world was filled with religious thought wherein deity was conceived as being present in the sphere in which mankind lives. Christianity marched forward into that world dynamically convinced that it was the herald of the "good news" that God had come in the person of Jesus Christ.

But, God had not only come into the world in Christ. The Divine which is transcendent and removed from man had become immanent to the degree that He had participated in the death which confronts all men. God in the person of Jesus Christ had demonstrated both His love for man and His involvement in the predicament of man by a deliberate act of Grace. It was Grace because it was not necessary; it arose out of the nature of God and was done because of divine intention and not divine necessity. Again, this was not something completely foreign to the religious thought world of the time of Christianity's beginnings. The Greco-Roman world was the scene of other religions which presented deities which died and rose from death. But in the Christian belief which combined the ethical monotheism of Judaism, the direct and close relationship of the Divine with an historical person, the death and resurrection of that person, and the assurance that all men who believe in and follow that person will participate in his triumph over death—in this belief the Christian religion possessed and presented a conception of the Divine which succeeded in bringing men to a consciousness and awareness of God which they had not known before.

The Christian presupposition concerning the nature of God has been of a dynamic character because of the strong belief that the Divine also is involved in history. We shall have occasion to discuss this at greater length in a later context, but no reference to the Christian belief concerning God is complete without mention being made of the degree to which Christianity has believed God to be a participator in history. Of course, this is not unique to Christianity. It is present in many, if not all, early forms of religion. In the religious experience of the Hebrew-Jewish people it reached a height which has only been equalled in Christianity and Islam. Both of these world-wide religions are the inheritors of the strong consciousness of the Jewish people that the Divine is taking an active part in the events which take place in the world.

God as the Lord of History is another indication of the degree to which the conception of the Divine as transcendent is qualified by the deliberate participation of the Divine in the affairs and concerns of mankind and the human dimension. It is not that God is not transcendent; rather, it is that by deliberate intent He qualifies that transcendence in order that man may achieve a state greater than he can attain by his own limited action. In some expressions of Christianity the involvement of the Divine in the affairs of the world has been held to include the most minute of events. In others the Divine has not been considered to be much more than the originator of the laws of nature and the determiner of the final goal of history. But, in either extreme God has been believed to be involved and concerned with the events which constitute human history and the individual well-being of men.

Christianity in its basic presuppositions concerning the nature of God has combined this belief in transcendence and immanence by its conviction as to the three-fold nature of the Divine. The Divine is revealed to man as "three Persons in one Substance." God is one, but in His activities and concern with the world and man He operates as the Father Creator, as the Son Redeemer, and as the Holy Spirit Companion of men. The trinitarian formulation of the nature of the Divine, of course, has given rise to some of the most involved formulations produced by Christian theology. Despite claims of critics that it has weakened, if not destroyed, Christianity's claim to being monotheistic, orthodox Christianity has insisted that God is one without essential division while at the same time holding firm to the belief that God has revealed Himself as three Persons.

A further word needs to be said concerning the Christian presuppositions about the nature of the Divine. Christianity shares with all religious experience in the difficulty of adequately stating in human terms its convictions pertaining to the beliefs it holds about the Divine and Its nature. Even where a basic presupposition exists that God has revealed Himself, those religiously sensitive men who have immersed themselves in the revelation are deeply conscious that the totality of the revelation is beyond adequate precise statement in human language. God is *wholly other* than man to the degree that human statements at best are only approximations of the full nature of the Divine. Human words and symbols can only suggest or indicate, they cannot be taken as identical with the Divine.

Nevertheless, Christianity has not allowed itself to degenerate as a result into a nebulous theory about the Divine without substance and concrete form. It has taken the teachings of Jesus and the early theological formulations of the Christian community as being the most adequate possible human statements pertaining to God. It has believed that these statements have been developed not only by the human mind, but they have been the result of a divinely initiated and guided religious experience. They may not portray God in His fullness; they do reveal God in a measure greater than the human words and symbols used because the Divine has participated in the religious experience from which they arise.

B. THE MUSLIM VIEW

The Muslim belief concerning the nature of the Divine, as is the situation in regard to many aspects of Muslim theological belief, is in part the product of the same religious ethos which produced Christianity. Islam is related to Judaism and Christianity as a result of its dependence upon them in its early theological formulations, as well as reflecting the same religious climate which produced the basic religious presuppositions which have characterized all three. Islam accepted the belief that the Divine had revealed Itself through the Hebrew people and their religious leaders; it recognized Jesus as being a prophet. In so acknowledging the supra-human nature of the religious knowledge possessed by Judaism and Christianity, Islam identified itself with much of the main outline of thought pertaining to the Divine which was fundamental to its two sister Semitic religions. However, in its belief concerning the nature of the revelation through the Prophet Muhammad and the Koran, Islam declared itself to be in possession of knowledge concerning the nature of the Divine which went beyond that to be found in both Judaism and Christianity.

A central conviction of Muhammad, and a presupposition which runs throughout the Koran, is that Allah is a Unity. This divine unity is not to be qualified in any way. Christian trinitarianism which suggests that God is divisible into Persons is not a pure monotheism in the Muslim view, and is to be rejected along with all other polytheisms. God is one and cannot be considered to be divisible even for purposes of understanding the variety of ways in which He has associated Himself with the world and man.

Philosophically, Islam has justified its presupposition as to the existence of Allah by its contention that nothing exists without a cause and that, therefore, there must be a Being which is the first cause of all that is known to man or experienced by him. This Being, Allah, exists of necessity as the starting point for all dependent existence, but is not of a dependent character Himself. He is self-sufficing, neither being dependent upon secondary existences such as the world, nor ultimately concerned with the final fate of the world.

Muhammad was convinced of the complete sovereignty of Allah over everything that exists. Allah is the complete despot in that all things are created by Him; their actions and fate are determined by Him, and He demands complete and absolute submission on the part of all that He has created. The power of Allah is paramount in any consideration of the nature of life and existence within the universe. Nothing is independent of that power in the sense that it can escape it or declare itself free from it. Everything, even that which appears to be acting contrary to Allah's power, ultimately is the result of the divine power.

In conjunction with the great stress laid upon the power of Allah, a power which is so overwhelming as to be terrifying and unapproachable, Islam confronts man with a divinity which is merciful and gracious. The despot who rules with an iron hand is also the Compassionate and Merciful Allah who is the guardian over all who submit to Him. He is the source of the material needs of His people. He is the deliverer of men from His own wrath which is reserved for those who do not submit to His sovereign power. As in Christianity, the Divine concerns Itself with man and his affairs through a gracious act or acts and not due to a necessity which would be an infringement upon the ultimate transcendence which is essential to Its nature.

Muslim theology has concerned itself with a penetrating investigation into the attributes of God. Insisting upon the absolute difference between Allah and man it has been confronted, nevertheless, by apparent anthropomorphic descriptions of Allah in the Koran. The orthodox position has been that the attributes of the Divine are beyond explanation and cannot be understood by finite man since they are in reference to the Infinite Divine. It is necessary that men should simply accept as divinely revealed that which the Prophet taught, content in the assurance that in submitting to the will of Allah as revealed through His chosen prophet they are fulfilling the Divine will. However, the inquisitive and sensitive religious mind is not content simply to accept. Along with that acceptance it seeks to know more by reflection and meditation. Some of the most beautiful and illuminating religious writings have arisen from the Muslim preoccupation with the attributes of Allah.

For the purposes of simplification we may mention three primary presuppositions concerning the nature of Allah. They are also to be found in Judaism and Christianity, and in most of the religious systems of the world. In the case of Islam, however, they are more forthrightly held and less qualified than in most other religions.

First, Allah is omnipotent. Being all-powerful, everything is completely under the governance of His power. We have already made reference to this presupposition concerning Allah as being basic to the thought of Muhammad and the Koran. No other religion has insisted so firmly upon the absolute unqualified nature of the Divine power. This power has no limits, no areas in which it is not operative absolutely and completely. This absolute power is related intimately with the will of the Divine. Allah can do whatever He wills. The will of Allah partakes of the power of Allah to the degree that whatever He wills comes to pass without qualification. Power and will are not separate, but are identical manifestations from the Unitary Divine Being which is the cause of all that is. Divine will is the directive element which guides the unlimited and absolute power, and both are primary attributes of Allah.

Secondly, Allah is omniscient. Allah knows all the past, the present, and the future. As His power extends to every sphere of existence, so too does His knowledge. This knowledge is not limited by space nor time; it is not subject to the boundaries of the dimensions which circumscribe man. There is no thought conceived by man which is not known, and known previously, by Allah. In fact, because of the power which is Allah's and the dependent nature of all existence upon Allah as first cause, such thought is itself the result of Allah's will and the imposition of His power. The fundamental presupposition of Islam that all is dependent upon Allah as its source logically produces the Muslim conviction that Allah is the possessor of all power and all knowledge.

Thirdly, and directly related to the two previous presuppositions, Allah is omnipresent. If everything exists as a direct result of Allah's will and power, and if nothing is that is not in the knowledge of Allah, it follows that Allah is everywhere. Allah is involved in all acts which occur since they take place only as a result of His directive will. Allah is present in all space or dimensions since such categories are dependent upon Him for their creation and continuation. However, caution must be given that the assumption is not made that the Muslim emphasis upon the omnipresence of Allah means that orthodox Islam is pantheistic. Allah is not in any of these things to the degree that they may be identified with Him. Allah's nature is so completely different from all that exists in the temporal-spatial realm that it is the greatest of heresies to make Him in any way correlative with existence itself. Rather, all that exists is dependent upon the Divine so completely that it cannot be explained nor understood apart from the Divine and Its creative sustaining activities which are operative everywhere. Allah must be present in all things or they would not be, but it does not follow that Allah is in any manner dependent upon that which He has created. The Divine is prior and determinative; that which exists is secondary and resultant.

Orthodox Islam has been determined throughout its history to raise Allah to such a position that His total otherness is never questioned. Muhammad's concern to overcome all polytheism and to establish Allah as the one and only deity supreme over all human and non-human existence led him to insist upon the complete qualitative and quantitative differentness of Allah from man. Allah is a Being without form and without parts, without beginning or end, without equal, and without associate deities. Nevertheless, such a Being must be described or referred to in terms which are used in the human sphere and which immediately suggest the very categories and limitations which must not be used. That which is beyond description must at least be partially described if it is to be at all apprehended by man. As a result of this difficulty, which is common to all religions in their discussion of the nature of the Divine, Islam boldly faced the issue by using human terms and categories while insisting that Allah does not partake of the categories which are used. Allah "hears" all sounds but does not possess an ear as men do. There is nothing which is, that is not "seen" by Allah but this must not be taken to mean that Allah has eyes as men have. Allah "speaks" and gives commands and promises but these are done without the organs of speech which are common to man. In all of these things the point of importance is the activity or ability and not the method or means by which it is done.

The Muslim presuppositions concerning the nature of the Divine are both simple and complex. They are simple in that they are straightforward in their demand of the Muslim that he believe in the totally sovereign, omnipotent, omniscient, omnipresent Allah portrayed in the Koran. They are complex in that they raise many intellectual questions which have intrigued Muslim theologians and philosophers throughout the centuries. The common man, as in other religions, has left these complexities to the intellectual, and the intellectual has produced some of the greatest works of theological speculation which have been produced by man. The consciousness of Allah in His fulness has given to the Muslim peoples a dynamic awareness of the place of the Divine in existence and human affairs which will not disappear in the foreseeable future. It has produced a religion and a culture which must be taken into account in any world-wide attempts to meet the problems of today and tomorrow.

C. THE HINDU VIEW

The Hindu presuppositions in regard to the nature of the Divine are many and varied if one takes the whole of Hindu religion into account. This is due to the lack of precise theological doctrine and dogma which we have noted. It has resulted in a variety of beliefs being present in the religious ethos which reflects the manifold nature of the Hindu religious experience. The Divine has not revealed Itself in one definitive and decisive event. It is not conceived as being perceived or understood by man in one form alone. It does not possess a certain set of attributes which restrict it from the possession of other forms and from every possible attribute. Hence, all conceivable beliefs concerning the Divine are to be found within the broad expanse of Hinduism.

However, if Hinduism has any cohesiveness at all other than the caste system, it is to be found in the philosophical-theological presuppositions which are common to the great majority of religious groups which go to make up Hinduism. Despite the great variety of interpretations, and in some cases outright rejections of these major theses, it is possible to come to some understanding of Hinduism and its vitality by an investigation of the fundamental theories which support the Hindu structure. These beliefs have characterized Hindu philosophical-theological speculation from an extremely early period in Indian history. They continue to be the major strands which hold together the Hindu view of existence.

The early Upanishads reflect thought which was current at the time of their composition some centuries before Christ, and indicate that even before their appearance Hindu thinkers had spent much time in speculation concerning the fundamental questions which reflective man asks. While it is important that we be aware of the existence of great and divergent variety within Hindu religion in its many sectarian expressions in both the past and the present, yet it is in the great philosophical-theological writings which Hinduism has produced, and upon which it continues to depend, that we shall find the fundamental presuppositions which make Hinduism what it is. The existence of schools of philosophy which have diverged from some of these presuppositions in radical fashion has not altered the general Hindu adherence to them.

Very early in the development of Hindu thought beyond primitivism there is the appearance of the conviction that there was a consciousness at work in the origin of the world. This consciousness, Brahman, had not only played a part in the past history of material existence, but It is the continuing power which pervades and upholds the total structure of the universe in the present. This Brahman is not to be confused with any of the deities in the early Vedas for even they are dependent upon It. The gods themselves are lifted to their high place in the structure of things by the power of Brahman.

In their attempt to fathom the nature of Brahman early Hindu speculators were deeply conscious of the mysteriousness and unknowability of the Divine. Early stories tell of the attempts of the gods themselves to understand the nature and character of Brahman. Convinced that Brahman pervades all of existence and that It is greater than any individual part of the whole of existence, religious thinkers developed a highly refined negative theology in which Brahman is said to be this thing and that thing until all possible physical material aspects of existence are mentioned. But immediately following such statements care is taken that it is understood that it is the creator and sustainer of these individual things which is the Divine, and not the things themselves. Brahman is to be found in particular phenomenal objects, but Brahman also transcends existent objects as no phenomenal substance is the basic stuff of creation, but is only a habitation of Brahman. All particular aspects of existence must be considered as referring back to a single unity or One "Who is the maker of these persons, of whom this (universe) is the work."

Brahman was early conceived as being a Soul (Ātman). Therefore, Soul is the source of all existent things, all vital energies, worlds, deities, all beings. This conception of the Divine as the source of all goes further by holding that the relationship between the Divine and Its creatures is of such an intimate nature that creation is dependent at all times upon its source. The source is not only necessary in the beginning moment of creation, it is just as necessary at every moment in which the creation exists. The Divine is the Real of the real. Brahman is the ultimate essence which constitutes the foundation or core upon which the apparent rests. That which appears to man to be real is only real in a secondary fashion. Its true reality is the Reality which is the Divine. It is apparent that we have here the beginnings if not the flowering of a pantheism wherein the Divine is present in all existence in more than a metaphorical sense.

The attempt of Hindu philosopher-theologians to ascribe to the Divine various attributes or characteristics was limited by the negative theology which we have just mentioned. As a result, any attempt to define Brahman in terms of human knowledge was futile in producing concrete presuppositions of the nature which we have discovered in Christianity and Islam. Whereas the other two religions recognize that the Divine is greater than the human understanding can fully grasp, Hinduism has insisted upon this so strongly that there has been less direct relationship between its intellectual theological formulations and the worship and beliefs of the masses. The Divine is essentially of a character or nature which cannot be grasped and communicated in the finite human realm.

The negative methodology employed by Hindu thinkers is well illustrated by statements similar to the following: The Divine is not in space; which is expressed by the assertion that It is infinitely large and infinitely small, that space is interwoven in It, and that It is all pervading. The Divine is not in time since it is not limited to the three categories of past, present and future. Brahman is of infinite duration for It is not born, does not die, and abides from everlasting. However, the Divine is of the instantaneous nature of the flash of lightning, or the swift rush of thought. The Divine is not causally dependent, and is absolute unity without diversity since It is independent of becoming and not-becoming, of good and evil, and of past and future.

A legend often used to indicate the nature of the Divine and the method by which It is to be known reveals the Hindu thinkers' insistence upon the ultimate mysteriousness of the Brahman. A philosopher is asked by an eager student as to the nature of the Brahman, but he remains silent and says nothing. He is asked again and again, but each stating of the question is met with silence. Finally, as the question is asked, the philosopher replies, "I teach you, indeed, but you understand not; silence is the Brahman."

Such intellectual speculations concerning the nature of the Divine are the foundation of orthodox Hinduism. In a later context we shall have occasion to enlarge further upon these presuppositions and their meaning and impact upon the general Hindu view of the nature of existence. However, it is clear to anyone who has even the most superficial knowledge of India that the vast majority of the Hindu people do not conceive of the Divine in such an intellectual and esoteric fashion. The presence in Hinduism of so many deities to be worshipped and acknowledged is, in a large measure, the result of the theological-philosophical insistence that the Divine is beyond human knowledge. For at the same time this insistence has been made, another current of religious thought has been running parallel to it in Hinduism. This is the strong conviction that the Divine is to be known by man in many forms and in all areas of experience. Brahman is not to be seen in Itself in these events, but religiously sensitive men are aware that the Divine is here and is at work. As a result, orthodox Hinduism has had a place for the many "minor" revelations of the Divine which have been experienced. In practice these revelations are individual deities who for the great majority of their worshippers are separate and distinct from the divine Brahman. In fact, they are very likely not at all conscious of the existence of Brahman. In theory, however, orthodox Hinduism looks upon these deities as creations of Brahman for the purpose of making Himself known to men of differing religious capabilities, or it tolerates such worship because it is convinced that the Divine is present in all forms of existence and any worship of whatever type is of value to man in his attempt to rise above his present limited state.

Modern Hindu apologists go to great lengths to make it clear that Hinduism is not a polytheism, and that it does not sanction idolatry. But, it must be understood that they are speaking from the standpoint of the educated intellectual Hindu who rationalizes such things from the perspective of the philosophical-theological tradition which is little known or understood by those who are engaging in apparent polytheistic and idolatrous worship. This is another instance of the tension to which we have pointed in the various religions between their higher and lower levels.

D. THE BUDDHIST VIEW

Buddhism exhibits a great variety of views in its presuppositions concerning the Divine. This is probably the most decisive point at which Buddhism is in conflict within itself theologically. The tension exists not only between southern Theravadin Buddhism and northern Mahayana Buddhism, but also within the two divisions themselves. Of course, it must be remembered that Buddhism, like Hinduism, has traditionally allowed a wide variety of thought in regard to many of the basic religious presuppositions which are the concern of men. Also, Buddhism did not originate out of a concern with the nature of the Divine, nor out of what was considered to be an action of the Divine. Rather, Buddhism in its first formative centuries was a religion with a message of how man might escape from the present existence which enslaves him. As a result, it was only in later centuries as the religion spread out of India and into the North that a concern with the nature of the Divine became of an importance similar to that in most of the other world religions.

The teachings of the Buddha regarding the nature of the Divine are of a two-fold nature. It has been popularly supposed by many that his thought was much like that of Confucius in China who stated that he was too concerned with the things about which he could know something to waste his time in speculation upon those things about which he could know nothing as long as he was a finite man. Such thought is to be found in popular legends and stories concerning both Buddha and Confucius, but in neither case do they get at the heart of the matter.

The Buddha was a reformer within Hinduism not only in his rejection of the accustomed and approved methods whereby men were to achieve salvation, but also in his rejection of the usual Hindu presuppositions concerning the Divine.

It was in this last point that he declared himself to be more than a reformer of Hinduism and, in reality, a founder of a new religion. It is true that he based his presuppositions upon a point of view which was present in Indian philosophy and which has continued to be a part of Indian-Hindu thought. But a deciding factor in the separation between Buddhism and Hinduism was the definiteness with which he incorporated his beliefs concerning the Divine into the whole of his scheme of salvation.

The Buddha's presuppositions concerning the Divine were negative. Deeply influenced by early expressions of what later flowered as Indian Samkhya philosophy, he held the universe to be constructed in a completely materialistic sense. The existence of a Divine was denied since everything was to be explained in terms of soul and matter. What is, is given and is without initial origin except that it is the compound and result of the pre-existent factors of soul and matter which are in interaction with each other. With the two given essences of soul and matter as the basic stuff of existence which is the result of the interaction of the two, there is no need for the intervention of a divine initiator or power.

Scholars in both the East and the West have engaged in many controversies over whether the foregoing is a correct understanding of the Buddha's position concerning the Divine. There can be little doubt but what he said very little if anything about God. The thought of the primitive Buddhist community as it is reflected in early Buddhist writings would seem to indicate that the predominate legacy concerning belief about the Divine which was left by the Buddha was a negative one which considered the Divine to be not unknowable by man, but unnecessary and consequently non-existent.

Southern Theravadin Buddhism has no consistent teaching on the subject of the Divine and Its nature. Seeking to keep itself true to early orthodox Buddhist thought on the matter while at the same time it came under the influence of the popular beliefs of the masses, Theravadin Buddhism has succeeded in reflecting the negative presuppositions of the Buddha only in theory but not in practice. Present-day intellectuals are insisting upon the atheism which they hold to be the correct Buddhist teaching. In the midst of the contemporary resurgence of Buddhism they are seeking to educate the youth in the philosophical and pyschological subtleties which have been lost by the masses of Southern Buddhism.

The popular polytheism of the Indian and southeast Asian peoples is evident in all of the areas of Theravadin Buddhism. We have mentioned previously the extreme difficulty a religion faces in overcoming the traditional and prevalent religious beliefs and customs of its adherents. In the case of Buddhism in many instances it appears that the absence of strict dogma has resulted in Buddhism being simply a veneer superimposed upon the religious customs of the people of its various areas. For the average Theravadin Buddhist there are many deities of varied characteristics. These deities are often limited in many ways as is man. Their attributes and powers are fearsome, lovable, and worthy of respect from man.

These deities often are not only limited in the same manner as man, but do not possess the high potentialities that are man's. They become old, lose their faculties, and may experience death. Like man they are subject to retribution or repayment for their deeds in past existences, and will enter after this existence into another stage. They are not in possession of complete knowledge, and may even be outwitted by men who know more than they. Subject to passions as are men, they are not possessed of unlimited power whereby they can escape the consequences of their passions and desires. In many respects they are of a sub-human nature since they cannot ultimately partake of the blissful salvation of Nibbana which is available to man.

Popular Theravadin Buddhism in practice has created a God out of the founder of Buddhism. The Buddha is considered to be higher than any of the deities which are known and worshipped or appeased by men. These gods pay homage to him in the same fashion as men do. The popular stories of the

birth, life, and death of the Buddha refer to the worship which
the gods offered to him. The Buddha is the instructor of the
gods in the same manner he is to men, and they are dependent
upon him for their salvation. Thus we see that in some cases
the gods are looked upon as being inferior to man in that they
cannot attain the Enlightenment of which the Buddha spoke,
and in other popular belief they are in exactly the same situation as men, and can attain it.

To the non-Buddhist observer it would appear that Theravadin Buddhism faces its greatest internal problem in its negative theoretical thought concerning the Divine. It is possible
for the scholar to hold to such presuppositions and to maintain a consistent philosophy upon which he can base his life
and actions. It is extremely difficult for the average person
to do so. The normal Sinhalese, Burmese, and Thai is aware
of the power which is in operation in the world and he is
driven to worship it. When he cannot find grounds for so
doing in the intellectual fomulations of his religion he naturally
turns to the beliefs and practices which he has inherited over
the centuries. He transposes the Buddha from an example and
teacher into a divine Being who for all purposes fulfils the
function of the Divine in the highest sense. He is to be
adored, and is the savior of men through the religious knowledge which He brought and demonstrated in His own Enlightenment.

Northern Mahayana Buddhism differs radically from
Theravadin Buddhism in its presuppositions concerning the
Divine. The original break between the two branches of
Buddhism arose to a large degree over their separate under-
standings of the nature of the Buddha. The scriptures which
have become the foundation of much of Mahayana thought
are filled with supra-human beings who are of a divine nature. There is no hesitancy to describe the nature of existence
beyond the human temporal-spatial sphere. It is basic to
much of Mahayana thought that in the last days of his earthly
life the Buddha revealed Truths concerning the nature of
existence beyond the human level. Mahayana is concerned,

therefore, with the nature of existence in non-human dimensions to a much greater degree than is Theravadin Buddhism. In fact, there are few religions which have erected as complex a hierarchy of divine beings as has Mahayana.

When we consider the Mahayana presuppositions concerning the fulfilment or salvation of man we shall see that in developing methods whereby man may escape from his present predicament Mahayana has placed special emphasis upon the existence of beings who serve as saviors and guides to man in his quest for fulfilment. These beings, though once men who were themselves involved in the human situation, have risen to a higher state of existence wherein they participate in a degree of divinity or Buddhahood. They are not *the* Divine, nor are they human with all of the limitations which that implies. It is because of the firm belief in the existence of these beings and the dependence of man upon them which Mahayana stresses, that Northern Buddhism has been forced to develop a complex theory of the nature of the Divine.

The religious knowledge which the Buddha is supposed to have revealed in the last stages of his ministry, and upon which most forms of Mahayana rest, depicts the earthly Buddha to be the Eternal Buddha who reveals himself in all worlds and existences. Gautama Sakyamuni, the earthly Buddha, is but one earthly incarnation of the Eternal Buddha who exists in countless worlds and in numberless periods of time. All things are subject to him; all worlds, their forms and inhabitants are the results of His creation. The Buddha of the great Mahayana scriptures partakes of all of the power and purpose which we have discovered in the Christian and Muslim theories concerning the Divine. Despite the fact that Buddhist psychology and theology usually continued to explain the world and existence in non-causal terms, Mahayana developed its scheme of non-monastic salvation upon the presupposition of a divine Being.

Theravadin Buddhism is often described as a system of "monastic salvation," while Mahayana Buddhism has preached "universal salvation." In its development as a missionary religion reaching into the many and varied cultural-religious areas of the Far East, Mahayana was forced to incorporate into itself the many deities which were an established part of the religious thought and customs of the people. These deities usually came to be recognized within the Mahayana theological system as sub-deities subordinate to the supreme Eternal Buddha. They are either Bodhisattvas who are striving to aid men in their attempt to escape from the limitations of human existence, or they are heavenly beings created by the Eternal Buddha for the purpose of running the universe and carrying out his will. In actual practice they have remained for many Buddhists as the deities who are most concerned with men and his problems. They are the objects of worship, rather than the Eternal Buddha who is so far removed from mankind and the consciousness of the average worshipper as to be almost non-existent.

By its policy of absorption of the many native local deities which existed in its path of expansion, Mahayana became a religion which contained within itself innumerable heavenly beings who fulfilled the part of the Divine for the common worshipper. There are few aspects of deity in human thought which cannot be found in some of the beliefs present in Mahayana Buddhism. In a similar fashion to that which exists in Hinduism, these various deities are tolerated by the more intellectual Buddhists as being necessary beliefs for those individuals who are not capable of grasping the more subtle aspects of involved Mahayana theology.

An interesting feature of Mahayana theology is the fact that the earthly Buddha, Sakyamuni, is usually subordinated in the divine hierarchy. Individual Buddhist sects or denominations have risen through the centuries placing special emphasis upon individual saviors or Bodhisattvas. These heavenly beings have come to be considered as more essentially or fully divine than the earthly Buddha. The earthly Buddha, along with them, partakes of essential Buddhahood, or Enlightenment, but in a lesser degree than they. All of these beings, along with the earthly Buddha, are divine, but they are at a higher stage of Enlightenment than he.

The stages or degrees of Buddhahood are numerous. All those beings who have been able to rise above the causal chain which produces sentient life in the physical dimension are now at some stage of Enlightenment. As such they participate in a degree of Buddhahood which fits into some level of the Buddha hierarchy in its broadest form. Technically, these various levels are radically different, and it is not proper in most instances to speak of a Bodhisattva as a Buddha. He has refused to take the ultimate step toward complete and full Enlightenment whereby he would be removed from perception by, or communication with, man. If he were to do so he would no longer be able to fulfil his function of aiding men in their quest for fulfilment or salvation. However, this is a theological subtlety which is not known by the average member of the Faith. For him these heavenly beings are the Divine who is to be worshipped and petitioned.

The philosophical metaphysical expressions and presuppositions concerning the nature of the Divine which are given by many forms of Mahayana are similar to those of most monotheistic systems. All existence, including the many deities, is the result of a First Cause or Principle. Popular religious literature and more sophisticated intellectual works do not avoid depicting this Principle in anthropomorphic and fanciful forms which are similar to highly symbolic and imaginative writings to be found in many of the religions. To the theologian the Eternal Buddha seated upon the Vulture Peak directing all worlds and adored by all creation in countless universes is the divine Principle pervading all existence. To the worshipper he is the Divine who is the source of existence and sustenance in the present, and the hope for fulfilment in the future.

It has been suggested that the conception of the Divine in Mahayana Buddhism is best understood by the formula or doctrine of the "Three Bodies" (Trikāya). Not all groups within Mahayana would subscribe in full to the doctrine, but it is helpful to a non-Buddhist in gaining insight into the general conception of the Divine and Its manifold nature. The lowest of the three aspects or categories of the Divine is the Nirmānakāya or "Condescension body." This is the form or manifestation of the Divine which was present in the earthly Buddha who lived at a certain time in the world. In Christian terms it may be described as the Divine incarnate in human life and history for the purpose of making the Divine known to men. The next category of the Divine is the Sambhōgakāya or "body of Bliss." This is the Divine in its capacity as God observable and knowable to mankind. The Sambhōgakāya fulfils the usual functions of God to be found in the popular beliefs of the leading religions of the world. It is the orderer and preserver of the universe. It is the Deity which is to be worshipped by man. The highest body or category of Buddhahood is that of the Dharmakāya or the "body of Truth." The Dharmakāya is the Ultimate First Principle. It is *the* Divine from which all things proceed and, as we shall discover, to which all things return. This is the ultimate Godhead which is so completely different from man, and so removed from him that It is only knowable by man in a secondary sense through the two subordinate bodies of Buddhahood. The three bodies are levels of Enlightenment with each higher level being further removed from the dimension of man, yet they are inherent in man as he now is as a phenomenal earthly being.

Those Buddhists who have suggested such a formulation are quick to point out that it must not be taken in a literal sense if the Mahayana presuppositions concerning the Divine are to be adequately understood. It is simply a convenient method whereby the various Buddhas which are present in the many groups of Mahayana can be classified as to their nature and function. The earthly Buddha is the supreme example of a Nirmānakāya, but there have been others in the eons of time in this universe and the countless other universes of the total of existence. The many deities or Buddhas of the heavenly hierarchy to be found in the areas of Northern

Buddhism are of the category of Sambhōgakāya; they are many and not one. It is only when we have come to the Dharmakāya that we have reached a monotheism in any sense of the word. Here we have a One to Whom all other manifestations of Buddhahood are subordinate. We have reached the level of theology and involved metaphysics which is understood only by the religious scholar and is hardly present in the mind of the usual adherent to the religion.

It remains to be said that Mahayana has a category of beings of a slightly lower stage in its intellectual presuppositions, which in practice fulfil the function of the Divine for the Mahayanist laity. These are the Bodhisattvas to whom we have referred. The religious man will not rest content with deities who are so far removed from him that they are only to be perceived through philosophic speculation or mystical intuition or enlightenment. In Mahayana the lay worshipper has found such beings in the Bodhisattva saviors who are the Divine towards whom he looks. These beings fulfil his religious needs and they give him the assurance he seeks in the midst of the confusion and struggles of human existence.

In our discussions of the presuppositions of the four religions concerning religious knowledge and the Divine certain similarities and differences have become apparent. For example, it is only in theoretical Theravadin Buddhism that a strict humanism concerning religious knowledge is to be found. If there is no Divine and yet ultimate Knowledge, Truth, or Enlightenment is obtainable to man, then it follows that man by following a certain method or path may obtain Truth as a result of his own efforts. However, we have indicated that such thought is held only by a very limited intellectual group of Theravadin Buddhists at the present time. In Christianity, Islam, Hinduism, and Mahayana a Divine is presupposed and in each case that Divine has initiated action whereby man can perceive Truth. Even in Hinduism, which has often been characterized by Westerners as being humanistic in its beliefs concerning religious knowledge, the Divine has acted and acts so that Truth may be apprehended by man.

The conflict between the religions on this point is basically a conflict of fundamental presuppositions and not of actual practice. These presuppositions are that the Divine has acted in a certain definite event or series of events in a unique qualitative degree not to be found in any other events in human history. Even the modern Hindu, who makes much of the various religions as being but different paths to the same goal, bases his thought upon what he considers to be the highest and most complete religious knowledge—the Vedas and their classical interpretations.

The existence of similarity must not obscure the definite conflict which exists. The fact that, with the single exception of some types of Buddhism, all the religions ultimately presuppose a unitary divine Being does not mean that such a divine Being is understood in the same or even a non-conflicting manner. It may be the initiator and sustainer of existence, but Its relationship with existence and Its meaning for man is different. And it is in the meaning of the Divine for man that religion is primarily concerned. Esoteric formulations of the nature of the Divine in Christianity and Islam have exhibited presuppositions as inscrutable as those to be found in Hinduism and Mahayana. But the Western religions are divided from the Eastern in the emphasis which they place upon concrete historical event in which the Divine has been decisively involved. For them the Divine is in relationship with men in recorded purposeful history; for the others both man and history are of a different character because of their beliefs about religious knowledge and the Divine.

IV. *THE CONFLICT*
BETWEEN RELIGIONS:
MAN AND HUMAN
FULFILMENT

Religion is concerned with man. For Christianity and Islam God is the fundamental fact of existence. Man is not the prime factor. He exists as a result whose ultimate purpose is to be understood correctly only in the light of his origin by the Divine. For Hinduism and Buddhism generally the secondary or derivative nature of man is not emphasized. Because of the close relationship, and often identification, of man and God, man is not primary since in the final analysis he does not exist as a separate being in one case, nor as an eternal identity in the other. We are faced, therefore, with the fact that in the leading religions of the world man as an individual eternal entity is not the primary fact of existence. If he is anything at all, he is of a secondary and derivative character.

Nevertheless, from the perspective of man, and in some instances from that of the Divine, man is of primary significance in the leading world religions. These religions arise from the fact that man is a creature who is not content with himself and his creaturehood, as well as from the belief that the Divine has approached man in self-revelation. Despite the high insights of religion wherein man has ceased to be concerned with himself and loses himself in dedication to the Divine, religion as a whole is the manifestation of man's concern with himself and his relationship to the ultimate meaning of his existence. A religion exists only because there are men who are religious. It has a basic function of bringing meaning and Truth to man. It is of primary importance in the world today because of man and his concern with his own fulfilment.

The foregoing is not to say that without man the Divine would not exist. But it is to emphasize that without man a consciousness of God would not be present in the world in a fashion which would be decisive. The existence of man may not logically necessitate the Divine, but to religious man his own existence has implied the Divine or at least a minimal structure and form to existence. The leading religions are confronting man today with the claim that they possess knowledge concerning the Divine, or the ultimate nature of existence, which is necessary to man if he is to understand himself correctly. They are insisting that contemporary man can only overcome his problems successfully if their separate messages are taken into account. They present conflicting messages and, therefore, seem only to add to the confusion of man. But for the vast majority of mankind they are the source of hope in the midst of confusion and despair.

The questions which man has asked and which have given rise to the great religions and philosophies of history indicate the centrality of man in existence. Man cannot conceive nor talk about an existence in which he himself does not play some part, or to which he does not have some relationship. The theological constructions of religions arise because man is constantly seeking that religious knowledge be meaningful to him. Man seeks to discover the meaning of his own existence and whether that meaning goes beyond the life to which he is now bound.

1. Man

The presuppositions which are concerned with the nature of *Man* in the various religions are beliefs which arise as a consequence of the theories concerning religious knowledge and the Divine. Indication is given regarding the nature of man by the manner in which he is considered to obtain knowledge of the Truth. The content of the Truth reveals what man is and what his divinely appointed destiny shall be. The purposes and attributes of the Divine which are made known in the religious knowledge are of prime importance to the religious believer because they are not isolated from man but, rather, are the fundamental reasons for man's existence. It is because the Divine is of such and such a character that man is to do one thing and not to do another. It is because the nature and will of the Divine is of one type and not another that the demands upon man in the world are what they are. It is because man is a creature resulting from the divine action that he is limited in his creaturehood as well as potentially something more. The four religions are in conflict concerning man as a result of their presuppositions about religious knowledge and the Divine. However, their conceptions of man are fundamental factors in their body of belief and are of primary importance in the conflicting claims which they present to the world today.

A. THE CHRISTIAN UNDERSTANDING

As in the case of the other basic presuppositions upon which it rests, Christianity is in debt to its Hebraic-Jewish heritage in the fundamental elements of its doctrine of man. Man is an individual being possessing uniqueness which sets him apart from all other creations of God, as well as separating each man from all other men. Early Hebrew religion gave to Judaism and to Christianity a consciousness of the social nature of man and of his relationship to the Divine which both religions continue to possess. But along with this awareness of man in community, the later Hebrew prophets came to realize the individual nature of man and of his relationship with the Divine.

Christianity has placed particular emphasis upon the individuality of man. Man is an individual who stands before God in his particular separate nature as a responsible being.

Man is in possession of a life which is his own and, therefore, occupies a unique place in existence. This uniqueness means that man is not to be confused with the Divine, nor is he to be confused with his fellow men to the degree that he is but one among the many and indistinguishable from the mass. This means that not only is every man responsible for himself and his actions in an ultimate sense, but he is required to recognize this individuality and responsibility in all other men. Christianity through its history has not always been true to this presupposition of uniqueness and ultimate responsibility and integrity of the individual. As an institution it has demanded conformity to a degree that the unique responsibility of the individual has often been overwhelmed by the pressure of the institution and society. Nevertheless, the human institutional and communal expression of Christianity has not erased the fundamental presupposition of the individual integrity and responsibility of men. In its best moments the institution itself has sought to develop such a consciousness within the men among whom it works.

At the same time that this individuality is stressed the derivative character of man must be emphasized. The individual man is an entity unto himself only in a qualified and not in an ultimate sense. For Christianity, individuality and uniqueness are eternal but they are qualified—qualified in that these attributes of man are not self-generated and without responsibility, but are derived and subject to a purpose outside and above man. The presupposition of the Divine which is fundamental to Christianity demands that man be viewed and understood from a perspective which is infinite and above man, rather than from a perspective which is finite and at man's level. Individual uniqueness with its accompanying dignity is a result of the Divine and Its purposes and actions. It is from God that these have come to man, and it is because of God that they have meaning and significance.

Man, the creature, is related to his source in a fashion which both limits his individuality as well as enriching it. The Christian message to mankind in its present predicament

is one which demands that men recognize this limitation. At
the same time it is a challenge to men that they rise to the
full stature which is possible for them as a result of their
relationship to the Divine which is their source of being.
The fact that man's individuality, uniqueness, and dignity
are derived is not limitation but enfranchisement. It is the possession of unlimited potentiality within the broad range of a
divine limitation which is so large in scope that it cannot
be viewed as limitation but only as opportunity.

Christian theology has been greatly concerned with the
biblical thought that man is created in the "image of God."
This has not been taken as having anthropomorphic meaning, but generally has been associated with the presupposition
that man in his ultimate nature partakes of a divine essence
which is not inherent in nor able to be possessed by the other
creations of the Divine. Man, therefore, stands in a relationship which is unique among all creatures and which en-
hances his dignity. However, the biblical concern with the
evil or sin which man commits implies a decay or loss of the
divine image in man. The "image of God" must always be
considered in the light of the "Fall of man" from his original
state of close relationship with God as portrayed in the biblical story of the Garden of Eden. Modern theological speculation in Christianity has emphasized that man as he now
is must be seen as a creature wherein that "image" has been
either lost or greatly diminished. Man possesses the "image
of God" only potentially and not actually, and it is the result
of the gracious action of the Divine and not of man's own
doing that he has it. But, the fact that man is not in the close
relationship with God that he could be is the result of his
own action and not of God's will. This points to the ability of
man to act contrary to the Divine and to separate himself
from the source from which he comes.

We are now at a central Christian presupposition concerning man. Man is a unique creature who possesses relationship to God which is not possessed by any other of the orders
or categories of creation. Because of his status as creature,

man is limited and finite and, yet, it is due to the peculiar nature of his creation that he possesses a potentiality unknown to all other creatures. Christian belief holds that this potentiality is a result of the bestowal upon man by the Divine of the capacity freely to choose between alternatives. Despite the fact that there have been those groups and thinkers within Christianity who have held that man does not possess "freedom of the will" in any final sense, the main stream of Christian thought, and the major groups of Christianity today, will not allow the responsibility of individual man to be put aside.

No creature is responsible if it is not able to make decisions independently of its Creator. If this responsibility is actual, it must be able to make decisions which are contrary to the will of the Creator. Those who are acquainted with Christian theology on this point will be aware of the involved nature of this problem and the many subtle arguments which can be made concerning it. For the main stream of Christian thought, no matter what involved theological-philosophical arguments have been given to the contrary, man has been able to declare his independence of God to a degree where he can stand as a pigmy defying a giant. This is sin in its true Christian meaning and the fact that the declaration of such independence is an illusion on man's part does not mitigate its seriousness. Man acting independently of the Divine is a pathetic figure who is confused by his own desires and conception of his uniqueness. Even his ability so to act is a result of a gift from God and, therefore, his defiant independence is a result of his own confusion and assumed self-importance. It is a delusion and is real only in the injury it does to man and to the relationship which God has established and seeks to enrich.

The evil nature which is to be found in man is the result of this ability to act independently of God. However, Christian theory concerning man has differed widely in its conclusions regarding the capability of man to act in accord with the divine will. Some of the leading thinkers of Christian history have held that man in and of himself is incapable of good as a result of the estrangement between God and man which is represented in the biblical story of the Fall of Adam. Others have not considered the Fall to have been of such a degree that man in his present state is completely immersed in evil and cannot at least approximate the will of God by good actions and good thoughts. Since Christianity holds that man in his original state of creation was in a relationship with God which has been lost and must be restored, the problem revolves around the question as to whether the loss is a complete one or only a partial one. In either case, the loss is conceived as being so great that divine assistance is needed in the restoration of the original relationship. And if any ability for good remains in man as he now is, it is still the result of the divine action and cannot be considered to be something created by man himself. Even the ability to choose between respective evils is the result of the divine gift of freedom and is not the outcome of human attainment.

There can be little doubt but that historically Christianity has placed more emphasis upon man's evil nature in his present state than upon his ability to do good. This is the result of the Christian conviction that the purpose of the unique revelation in Christ was to restore the broken relationship between God and man which is the result of man's misuse of his freedom and the cause of his evil thought and action. The message of Christianity is that man is now in a sinful or evil state but that condition can be overcome by the re-establishment of the proper relationship between God and man through man's acceptance of the teachings and work of Jesus Christ the Son of God. Periods of emphasis upon the sinful nature of man in Christian history have been followed by movements which have insisted that man in Christ is restored to his rightful and great place as a child of God. Both currents of thought have gone to extremes which tend to obscure the truth of the insight of the other, but neither in and of itself alone can be considered to represent the full Christian understanding of man.

We shall be concerned in our next section with a discussion of the Christian presupposition concerning the future state of man and his fulfilment. However, at this point it is necessary to mention that the immortality of man is a cardinal principle in Christianity. It is certain that the impact of the teachings and life of Jesus upon his early disciples was one which convinced them that man will exist in some state beyond the present one. The New Testament reflects thought concerning the future life which was current among certain groups of Jews as well as among other peoples of the Eastern Mediterranean world. Whether such an existence would be in a heaven outside this world or whether it would be in a future Kingdom of God in this world may be debated by scholars. The point, however, is that Christianity has held firmly to the conviction that a central factor in the religious knowledge brought to man by Christ is that it is the will of the Divine that man exist in a meaningful relationship to Him after the experience of death.

Man the creature of God is independent and unique, but he is always dependent upon God for that freedom and that individuality. He is caught in a situation of his own making because he has turned his independence to his own ends and forgotten his derivative nature. He can dream great dreams and establish societies for their fulfilment, but it is the Christian conviction that these hopes and endeavors are doomed unless the true understanding of the nature of man and the purposes of the Divine are integral parts of human society and individual consciousness. Human society and individual men are doomed to frustration and self-defeat unless the relationship between the human and the Divine which gives man and his society meaning is re-established through the agency of Christ.

B. THE MUSLIM UNDERSTANDING

The Muslim presuppositions concerning the nature of man share in a very limited degree with the views of Christianity which we have just discussed. This is due primarily to the

common early Hebraic heritage which the two religions share
rather than to an outright adoption by Islam of Christian
thought. However, the Muslim belief regarding man is not
at all to be identified with Hebraic-Jewish conceptions. It
merely assumes the relationship between man and the Divine
which is revealed in the Old Testament and does not appear
to reject the general presuppositions concerning human
psychology which are to be found in Hebraic thought.

Islam derives its central convictions concerning man from
its theories regarding the nature of the Divine. Our discussion of Muslim views of Allah has indicated the extreme
degree to which the sovereign absolute nature of Allah is
emphasized. As a result Muslim theories of man must always
be considered in relationship to the Islamic conviction that
all that is derives its nature from the sovereign Divine whose
power is in no way limited by Its creations nor by Its own
intention. As in Christianity and Judaism man is a creature.
For Islam, this creaturehood is the central fact about man in
a degree even surpassing that found in the other two religions. The limitations which creaturehood places upon man
generally are more restrictive in character than that found
in the other two religions. In any system of thought, creaturehood is meaningless unless the nature of the Creator is taken
into account. For Islam, the accepted beliefs about Allah, the
Creator, are such that any discussion of man is ultimately lost
in a consideration of the Divine.

The nature of individual human life in the temporal sphere
is not only determined by the nature of that which surrounds
man as a result of Allah's act of creation. At every moment
it is determined by the sovereign will of Allah. All events
experienced by man are moments which fall within the foreknowledge of the Divine. The absolute power of Allah is
operative in every sphere of activity, human or non-human,
which can be conceived by man. There is nothing at any time
or any place in existence or non-existence which is separate
from Allah's will, power, foreknowledge, or intent.

The question of "freedom of will" early appeared in Muslim theological speculation and controversy. The Koran itself evidences little concern with the problem. Like the New Testament it is not an attempt at systematic theology but, rather, is concerned with presenting a message of divine revelation. Muhammad was concerned with confronting men with the necessity to repent and submit to the sovereign God. The fact that he would feel that such a challenge should be presented, and that he thought of men as being able to respond to it, indicates that he believed men to be creatures with a power of choice. However, the portrait of Allah which is presented in the Koran is one which forced later theologians to come to the conclusion that even on this point Allah's will was the supreme factor in the matter, and not man's capacity to respond. Such a conclusion was not arrived at without intense theological struggle within early Islam. Conflicting parties and schools of thought produced some of the most interesting theological-philosophical systems in their efforts to solve the problem. The conclusion of the matter, as we have indicated, was one which ultimately was decided on the basis of Allah's complete sovereignty and man's total dependence upon his Creator.

Despite constructions of thought which seek to maintain the absolute and total sovereignty of the Divine while placing responsibility upon man, anyone approaching the Muslim solution to the problem from outside cannot escape the conclusion that, if man is responsible, he is without any real opportunity to exercise that responsibility. Freedom of the will does not exist in any system of Muslim thought which would be recognized by any representative body of Muslims. Allah decrees all that is, or happens, or can happen. He places responsibility for all events or decisions upon those men who participate in them, though the initiatory action and the inevitable consequence are determined and known to Allah. What man wills is caused by the Divine and is known by the Divine before it is cognitively present in man. Allah is responsible for all, and all is derivative from Him.

It immediately will be apparent that this implies that both

good and bad are the results of Allah's will. Allah is responsible for that which even appears to be in direct contradiction to His will and purposes as men conceive them through the religious knowledge which they have received from Allah. On this point Muslim theologians have given an answer which is found in other systems which are confronted with the same problem as a result of their insistence upon an Absolute Divine which creates and dominates all that exists. Allah, they hold, creates all, and any aspect of existence which appears to be acting in opposition to the Divine will or purpose is only doing so in a secondary, and not in a primary sense. That is, the supposed contrary action is apparent only and is not actually so. It is apparent from the limited finite view of man, but from the Divine perspective it is but one part of the total purpose of creation and existence. The ways of the Divine are not to be questioned by man, for they are beyond his comprehension. What the Divine decrees is good and bad only from the limited perspective of man. Ultimately, no such distinctions can be made.

Since the foregoing is fundamental to Muslim presuppositions regarding the Divine it follows that man is caught up in the purposes of Allah without possessing a uniqueness which results in freedom of choice and self-determination. Where in Christianity that self-determination is limited by the derivative and limited character of man, for Islam it would appear to be completely absent because of an absolute dependence and more restricting limitation. Muslim thought differs at this point in that the Divine is not conceived as conferring on man something of Its own nature. The "image of God" concept has not played the part in Muslim theory that it has played in Christianity. Groups within Islam have held that there is a spark of the Divine in particular men; some have placed emphasis upon the koranic statement that Allah is in the heart of every believer. But such beliefs have not been able to develop into a conception of man as an independent being of dignity and character who as a result of his own will can assume a position in direct opposition to the

Divine. Where Christianity's concern with man's dignity as a child of God has appeared at times to place limitations upon the Divine, Islam's concern with God's sovereignty has appeared to create restrictions upon man of such weight that man is of no consequence.

Such generalizations do not do justice to either of the religions. In both of them extreme positions at either end of the matter are to be found. Orthodoxy has usually adopted a middle ground which has emphasized the will and power of the Divine while not ignoring the responsibility which falls upon man. For all practical purposes the individual man in Islam is called to account as to whether he submits to Allah and is a Muslim or not. In the worldly sphere he is a responsible being and must make choices. The difference lies in the fact that Islam has given stronger support to the human tendency to accept what is and what comes as being the result of divine will. Kismet, fate, or destiny, plays a greater part in human thought in the Muslim world than it has done in Christian history. For the Muslim, man cannot stand in opposition to God because no action is possible without divine support. For the Christian, man can stand in opposition to God even though in so doing he is defeating himself.

Again, it is necessary to understand that the practical aspects of religious living have greatly qualified the fundamental presuppositions of Islam. The deeply religious layman is not concerned with whether what he does is determined by Allah or not. What does matter to him is that he can be conscious that the powerful and sovereign God is protecting and guiding him in what he does. Islam has given to its adherents a deep conviction that Allah is merciful and compassionate at the same time it has emphasized the justice and wrath of Allah. The more involved presuppositions of the Faith have not been the concern of the pious non-intellectual believer. Throughout its history Islam has produced sects and individuals who have lived with the conviction that because of His compassion and mercy Allah is closer to them than the

air they breathe. And in such close proximity there
is companionship and love as well as sternness and justice.

Our subsequent discussion of the Muslim presuppositions
concerning the fulfilment of man will indicate the application
of the beliefs concerning the compassionate gracious nature
of Allah to the most pressing concerns of mankind. Only the
most discerning and involved discussion of Muslim theology
in all of its many facets would do justice to the strengths of
the Muslim call to submission to Allah and His sovereignty.
Western non-Muslim scholars have often become so involved
in the basic presuppositions of Muslim thought that they
have assumed Islam to lack a fundamental warmth and affection for the Divine, or have assumed it to be present only in
Sufism and the Muslim Brotherhoods. But it must be made
clear that any interpretation of Islam which insists upon the
absolute transcendence, power, and sovereignty of the Divine
without also recognizing the fundamental importance of the
intimate relationship between Allah and the believer is not
adequate nor correct.

An important consequence of the Muslim conception of
Allah and the nature of man is the strong place Islam has
for the conception of the relationship between men within
the Faith. The Brotherhood of Believers is one of the outstanding characteristics and strengths of Islam. This is a
result of koranic teaching as well as of the early community
character of Islam. It has been perpetuated through the centuries by theological thought, theoretical Muslim religious-
social-political unity under the Caliphate, and by the consciousness of intimate personal relationship that is present
among any group of worshippers who are bound together by
certain common fundamental beliefs and customs. It is a
theory which is present in more than one religion and which
is to be observed in practice in all religions to some degree.
However, Islam has been more deeply conscious of it than
any other religion and, in the opinion of many observers, has
continued to exemplify the close relationship between men

of faith and consciousness of God in a manner not attained by any of the other leading religions.

Of course, there are many examples in Muslim history of internecine strife and group class consciousness. Theory is not always a part of practice in any religion. For Islam, however, the consciousness of the equality and community of all who are of the Faith is a dynamic which cannot be stifled. In the eyes of Allah each man possesses an equality of worth and a place in the scheme of things which places him on a par with others. By His actions, wherein one is lifted to high station and another is destined for lesser things, Allah is showing a favoritism which may in the next instant be reversed. Each event in human history arises out of Allah's will, and Allah is as important in the life of the lowest man and his destiny as He is in the life of the Caliph.

This belief in the Brotherhood of the Faith is evidenced in the strong insistence in Islam that the voice of the community has validity in interpreting the will of Allah and the content of religious knowledge. In part this is an inheritance from the nomadic Semitic background out of which Islam comes. But even more fundamentally it is the result of a strong belief that Allah has chosen certain men, those who submit to Him, to be witnesses of Him and His Truth. Those who are so engaged are bound in a fellowship which is cemented by the power of the sovereign God. They have a responsibility to each other which is animated by the divine will. They are a community which rests upon Allah's will and His promises. They are bound together by His revelation that such is His will for all who submit to Him.

C. THE HINDU UNDERSTANDING

The Hindu beliefs concerning the nature of man are best stated in the great philosophical-theological literature upon which we have been dependent in our previous discussions of Hindu thought. As in every other aspect of Hindu belief, we are confronted by the problem of ascertaining the fundamental presuppositions of a heterogeneous mass of belief which varies from religious group to religious group. The intellectual formulations of thought do not always reflect the beliefs upon which the average believer bases his life, nor are they representative of thought of which he himself is necessarily aware.

However, here again it is possible to distinguish in the orthodox formulations of Hinduism a fundamental core of presuppositions which may be said to be typical of Hinduism in most of its manifestations. The fact that there are many within the religion who are not consciously aware of them in more than a minor degree does not erase the fact that they are fundamental to the over-all system of which the average Hindu is a part. Even the differences between groups in Hinduism are variations upon these basic presuppositions.

We have seen that the Hindu conception of the Divine is one wherein the Divine is considered to be of a nature which is all-inclusive. The Divine is related to all that is at the same time It is held to be beyond all that exists. While insisting that the Divine can only be perceived in a negative fashion in realms of human rationality, Hindu thinkers have held the Divine to be present in the sphere of human existence to a degree not found in any of the other major religions. Side by side with the development of the theory that the Brahman is by nature beyond human description there was also the growth of the conception of Brahman as being manifest in an individual person's psychical activities. Brahman is to be found centered in the sense organs and the mental organs of man. The various qualities which were ascribed to Brahman were qualities which men knew to be also the property of the human self. Intelligence, truthfulness, blissfulness, and steadfastness were held to be intimately related to Brahman, if not actual aspects of It. As a result, through the centuries of theological development Brahman came to be considered as the "Self" which is without limitation.

In the Upanishads human speech was held to be a manifestation of Brahman since it makes the sciences, all objects, and all distinctions known. But, since it is the mental organ of the mind which embraces speech and conception, the mind is also Brahman. By involved philosophical argument it is demonstrated that everything is mind; the self is mind, the world is mind, and Brahman is mind. A step is taken beyond the category of the mind by demonstrating the existence of the "will" or the constructive faculty. Everything comes into existence through "will." "Will" defines a phase of Brahman, but there is still something greater—"thought." It is only as one "thinks" that "will" results. It is from "thought" that the various processes of existence result, and all of these processes as well as the initial "thought" are to be identified with Brahman. In its theory of the Divine, therefore, Hinduism identified the Divine with all phenomena—material and non-material.

In developing a theory of man, Hinduism was not only influenced by this identification of the Divine with all perceivable existence. As we indicated in a previous discussion, Brahman was also conceived in some sense as a Soul, an essence which is in some manner to be related with the finite ego of man.

The word *Ātman* was early used in the Vedas to refer to the ultimate essence of the universe. It was also used to denote the vital breath in man. In the later speculative writings the word came to be reserved in most cases to indicate the inmost essence within man, while the term Brahman is set apart to suggest the ultimate essence of the universe. However, the philosophical-theological literature is emphatic in declaring that the two are one and the same. Ātman equals Brahman, and Brahman equals ātman.

This inmost essence of man, the ātman, lies deep within him. Beneath the covering of the body there is another self which is distinct from the physical. This is the self which is the vital breath of man. This self, however, is the outer covering for another self, the will. Probing further within the will there is to be found the self which consists of consciousness, and so on. The ultimate self, the final essence of man, is self as pure bliss. Seeking to discover the constant and unchangeable essence in man which is without limitation, the great Hindu thinkers of the past were driven to such descriptions as "pure subject-object-less consciousness," "the reality," and "the bliss." This inmost essence of man, the ātman, is the seer of all seeing, the hearer of all hearing and the knower of all knowledge. The ātman sees but is not seen, hears but is not heard, knows but is not known. The ātman is like a lump of salt with no inner or outer, which consists through and through entirely of savor. The ātman consists through and through entirely of knowledge.

Bliss is not an attribute of the ātman. Rather, the ātman is bliss itself. The state of Brahman, *the* ultimate Ātman, is like unto the state of dreamless sleep. The human person who has reached this bliss is beyond fear. The ātman is dearer to the human being than any possession or any beloved person, for it is for it and by it that things appear dear to us. Man's inmost ātman is, therefore, the dearest of all that is dear. Since the physical is bound by limitation and all limitation is filled with pain, it is in the infinite alone that there is the highest bliss. When a man receives this rapture, this inmost ātman, then he is full of bliss. Man has attained peace when he comes to know that his inmost being is the invisible, supportless, inexpressible, unspeakable *One*. The inmost ātman which is his ultimate essence is the ultimate essence of all that is, the Brahman. As one Upanishad puts it:

And verily this Self is the lord of all beings,
the king of all beings. And as all spokes
are contained in the axle and in the felly of
a wheel, all beings, all gods, all worlds, all
breathing things, are contained in that Self.

A philosophical Monism, or Oneness, is the ruling conception of all creation. The world or universe and all that is in it is identical with *the* Ātman or Brahman. When considered in terms of his inmost essence man is to be seen as Brahman— the Divine. The extreme expression of this unity or identity is the phrase "That art thou" (*tat tvam asi*).

The foregoing will indicate the concrete manner in which early Hindu philosophy established an identity between the Divine and man. When man seeks diligently to discover what is his inmost nature he comes to realize that it is identical with the ultimate essence of all existence—Brahman. Man's ātman or self is the same as the divine Ātman or Self. The two are one and the same. There is no differentiation to be made between them.

The presupposition of the identity of man with the Divine which has been described is associated with the interpretation of the Upanishads made by one of the greatest figures in Hindu history—Shankara. It must be realized that other individuals and groups have interpreted the Upanishads in differing ways. However, the underlying presuppositions of orthodox Hinduism concerning the nature of man are revealed in the thought of Shankara even though his interpretation has not been accepted by all branches of Hinduism. Many levels of Hindu theological thought and practicing belief may reject it, but in so doing they do not escape its influence. At almost any level of Hinduism above the lowest forms of animism the all-pervading nature of the Divine is firmly presupposed. All existence is intimately related to, or is identified with, Brahman. And man is no exception to the rule.

The question remains as to why it is that man—who ultimately is closely related to, if not of the actual essence of the Divine—is in the predicament in which he finds himself? Life is conflict and struggle. It is seldom bliss. Even when man is able to rise above the common and usual limitations he is aware that the bliss he experiences is but momentary and not enduring. Such experiences are neither permanent nor completely satisfying, for their satisfaction is limited by their fleetingness. Man's ultimate divinity would seem to be of no real consequence because of man's limitation.

Hinduism has not ignored such problems. On the contrary, the basic presuppositions of Hinduism have been concerned with them. At the risk of anticipating our discussion of the Hindu beliefs concerning human fulfilment, it is necessary to consider briefly the Indian presuppositions concerning the nature of existence and the human perception of the material world.

As a result of their theories concerning the nature of the Divine, Hindu thinkers very early came to the conclusion that the world or universe is not real in the full sense of the word. Nothing within the physical experience of man ultimately possesses a truth of its own, because its final reality is a property of the Divine. Man does not experience through his senses anything that is Real. He is confronted only by external manifestations of the Real, and the manifestations may be considered Real only in a secondary sense. In a fashion similar to Platonic thought, or to that of Kant in Western philosophy, it is only the "ideal" behind the imperfect manifestation which is Real; the "thing in itself" is never fully comprehended by human observation. The use of small and capital letters in the writing of the same word is helpful in that it serves as a reminder that one conception of Real is in an ultimate sense, and the other conception of real is in a secondary connotation. The material, empirical universe must be considered real by man for the purpose of his own existence. But, this reality must not be confused as being the Reality which is continuing and unchangeable. At this point we are approaching the eternal problem which confronts theology and philosophy—the great inadequacy of words to convey the full meaning of human thought. Hindu speculation in its endeavor to make it clear that there is a difference between absolute final Reality and finite changing reality has often been misunderstood by non-Hindus. Of course, the difficulty of translation of the full thought of a word from Sanskrit to a European language has not made the problem any easier.

The germ of the later highly developed theory of *māyā* is to be found in various passages in the Upanishads. Māyā has been interpreted or translated by European scholars to mean "illusion," "non-real," and so on. As was suggested in an earlier connection and in the preceding paragraph, the point at issue is best understood by the use of the term "secondary reality." In their attempt to arrive at the Divine, the early Hindu thinkers were driven to reduce all so-called reality ultimately to Reality only. All things were presupposed to be simply modifications of true Reality. Convinced that the only Real is that which is beyond causality, which does not change, and which is without limitation, they came to the conclusion that all that is subject to causal effect from something other than itself cannot be held to be Real in any significant manner. Therefore, all that can be experienced by man and can be perceived by his senses is not Real, since it is subject to change by causes outside itself and is limited by its apparent characteristics. The illusory nature of empirical reality is established, therefore, since it obviously does change and suffers limitation.

If this be so, how, then, can that which exists be said to be existent in any final sense? Man is placed in the midst of such existence; in fact, he is a part of it. Is he to commit himself in dependence upon that which is not actually Real? If he does not do so, how can he sustain himself in the actual problems of life which confront him? The answer given by Hindu thought has been, generally, that it is at this point that man makes the mistake which results in his being bound to human existence with its problems and sufferings. Man is convinced that that which he experiences is Real. He does not understand it for what it is—secondary reality which when compared with the divine Real is illusion. Man's predicament arises from the fact that he concludes that what he experiences through his senses is Real and places his attachments and desires upon it. The Real which is what he truly seeks is the source of the real that man experiences, but man does not penetrate the real in order to confront that which is his goal. Man is confused into thinking that he has discovered the Real, whereas in actual fact he has stopped at Its manifestations.

The human predicament, therefore, arises because man's nature is not rightly understood. At all but its lowest levels

Hinduism is convinced that much of the human tragedy is a result of the confusion of the world with the Ultimate. It is a subtle philosophical-theological problem and it is a very actual religious concern at the level of the intelligent worshipper. The presuppositions of Hinduism concerning man are both conflicting and complementary at this point. Man, who at his innermost essence is indistinguishable from the Divine, is himself caught in a situation where he confuses the Divine with that which is only a manifestation of the Divine.

The apparent inconsistencies which our discussion of Hinduism's presuppositions may have suggested must not be considered to be unnoticed by Hinduism. Hinduism has produced some of the most subtle and involved philosophical-theological writings and schools of thought known to man. In claiming that all is One in the Divine, and that existence as perceived by man is not Real, Hindu thinkers are not being inconsistent as might appear to the mind untrained in philosophy. The great number of differences that seem so real in experience are not composed of the inner being of the One. They are an appearance, a phenomenon. Reality is One and Unity, while diversity and manifoldness are only an appearance. The formed and phenomenal Brahman is unreal. Brahman is Real only in formlessness and non-phenomenality.

It is interesting to Christians to note that Christianity has made a similar emphasis upon the confusion that man makes between the valuable and the non-valuable, the Real and the non-Real. Possessing a completely different view of the world, Christianity has, nevertheless, emphasized that one of the major roots of man's troubles lies in his confusion of material existence with eternal values. Christianity does not carry this thought to the extent arrived at by Hinduism, but it does underline the limitations of man's perception of the Divine and his confusion of his material surroundings with the ultimate ground of his existence.

The foregoing discussion of Hindu presuppositions concerning man should indicate the dependence of Hinduism upon its conceptions of the Divine. For a completely different reason from that of the Semitic religions, the Divine is the determining factor in arriving at a belief concerning man. Where in the other two religions the Divine is to be understood as being separate and distinct from the world of existence, though concerned with it, in Hinduism the Divine is held to be the world itself though not identical with it. Man, for the former, exists as a separate entity created by the Divine but not identifiable with It, while in the latter, man's distinction from the Divine is an illusion which is the result of ignorance as to the true nature of things as they ultimately are.

D. THE BUDDHIST UNDERSTANDING

The Buddhist conception of the nature of man is one of the most subtle and refined systems of thought which have been produced in any area of human speculation. The Buddha revolted against the accepted Hindu thought of his time in his strong denial that there is an ātman or self in man which is eternal and is distinguishable from the physical aspects of man. The Buddhist presupposition in this regard has been termed the *Anatta* or "no-self" doctrine. Traditional interpretation of Buddhist thought has centered around the conception of the apparent self as being nothing more than the manifestation which appears as a result of the composition of the five aspects which go to make up the individual man. Buddhism analyzed the individual man as being the composition of aspects called *khandhas*. These five factors are impermanent and the permanence which seems to be discernible is only a momentary apprehension of the separate aspects in temporary association. A traditional Buddhist figure used to explain the belief is that of a chariot which cannot be said to be more than a collection of its separate parts. The chariot does not exist apart from the individual aspects which collectively produce it, and when any one of the parts is taken away the remainder is not a chariot. In the case of man it is demonstrable that the individual parts and functions which constitute man as he is perceived in life fade away and disappear in death. There is nothing permanent to continue because there was nothing permanent to begin with nor has anything permanent been produced in the course of life.

One exception has to be made to the preceding statement. Buddhism was declaring that there is no continuing substance or eternal self which exists in the individual man. There is only the existence of the convergence of factors, an existence which is in the moment of their meeting but which ceases upon their separation. However, Buddhism did seek to maintain that there is something which is passed over from one existence to another in the many rounds of existence which were presupposed by Hinduism and by Buddhism. At the same moment Buddhism was denying the concept of self which was so fundamental to Hinduism, it was also maintaining that total annihilation does not result from the scattering of the separate aspects of individual man at death. Man and his appearance as an entity is impermanent; he is momentary. Nevertheless, that which is momentary is the result of causality. Nothing is passed from one complex of separate aspects to another complex but cause or compulsion.

This presupposition is explained by Buddhism in its theory of "dependent origination." Holding that man is not the possessor of a permanent self which continues through the separate and many existences which are the lot of man, and denying that all results from the existence of the individual are annihilated, Buddhism concluded that what does continue beyond the momentary association of aspects are causes which result in the origin and nature of the next association of aspects. The man who is reborn is not the man who has died, but he cannot be said to be different from this man. He is the result of the previous man; the result of his actions, though he is not in any manner the reconstitution of the previous aspects of the now dead man. Therefore, there is no ego or static essence which continues from one existence to another. There is no entity, man, which manifests itself in each existence which it undergoes and which is the same in each one. On the contrary, Buddhism is emphasizing the conviction that human life is a continuing series of causes and effects wherein each existence is the effect of the preceding existence and the causes which it set in motion.

As in the case of the Hindu doctrine of *māyā* concerning the nature of the physical world, it is necessary at this point in our discussion to mention the Hindu and Buddhist presupposition which has resulted in the doctrine of Karma. Very early in the development of Indian religion it was concluded that every individual receives reward or recompense for his good and bad actions in this life in future states of existence. Scholars differ over whether this belief preceded or followed the development of the theory that the individual passes from one life to another in the world rather than proceeding from this existence to another in some other world or sphere. Among the masses of Hinduism and Buddhism there is still strong belief that even though man may go through endless series of lives here on the earth there are periods when, as a result of his actions on earth in one existence, he spends some time in a heaven or hell in recompense. Nevertheless, both Hinduism and Buddhism have been wedded to the presupposition that life continues in a series of births and rebirths which are effected by the actions of the individual in previous existences.

As an offspring of Hinduism, Buddhism has continued in this belief. However, since it denies the existence of an entity such as the self or ego, what is it that is passed over from one existence to another? It is the series of causes and effects which result from one convergence of the five separate aspects of the individual, and which on the dissolution of the association of aspects cause the emergence of a new association of aspects. The cause which is put in motion by one association makes its appearance in the rise of a new convergence of aspects. Man, therefore, is always the result or the effect of a previous cause. It is only in this sense that he may be said to continue from one existence to another. Man is the product of his own action in the past, and will be what he will be in the future as a result of his actions in the present.

Karma, or the Law of the Deed, is a fundamental presupposition of Buddhism and Hinduism. It is an essential part of their beliefs concerning human fulfilment as well as their doctrines concerning man and his nature. For Buddhism it means that man as he is now in this existence is the result of what he has been in the past. In fact, the only thing which causes him to experience or know life in this or any other existence is his previous action. There is no material or spiritual substance which must be continued or which would disappear if the individual were not to undergo more lives. In fact, the individual is but momentary himself and only his actions and their effects are continuing—though they also may be snuffed out, as we shall see in a later context.

The Buddhist doctrine of man leaves us with the present existence of a being who is of concern to himself both now and in the future. He is concerned with himself now so that he may obtain pleasure and escape suffering in this existence, and he has concern for the future in his desire that it may not be more painful than pleasing. For all practical purposes the denial of the existence of a continuing self makes little difference between the everyday affairs or thought of the Buddhist and the Hindu. Their common acceptance of the presuppositions of Karma and resulting rebirth leads them both to primary concern with the method whereby Karma and its resulting fruits may be overcome.

It would appear on first glance that the theory of man in Buddhism would inevitably result in a strong belief in a fate that cannot be escaped. It is certainly true that Buddhists are committed to the thought that their present state and actions are the result of causes from the past. However, for Buddhism these are not finally determinative and absolute. Fate is not something which is to be submitted to without protest or hope of escape. The situation in the present and in the future for man is dependent upon man. Man is not the completely helpless victim of something outside himself which he cannot control or resist. The aspects which now constitute his total being are new and different from those which have existed before. At each level of existence he is in possession of will and purpose which he may use to determine his own fate by shaping his own future Karma. Karma for the future is caused by the individual in the present, and, though the state of the present is related to causes from the past, the will and purpose of the individual are not completely bound nor absolutely limited by it. It is because of this freedom in the midst of causality that Buddhism can present a message of salvation and human fulfilment. By the adoption of the proper method, man, the result of inescapable cause, can bring about the cessation of the cause.

2. Human Fulfilment

The presuppositions of the great religions concerning the destiny of man, or what we shall call *Human Fulfilment,* are the result of the previously discussed theories regarding the Divine and man. The religious knowledge claimed by each of the religions reaches its summation in the message it contains concerning human fulfilment. The message reveals the nature of God, the nature of man, and the reasons for man's present predicament. For the Western religions it makes known to man the divine purpose and plan whereby man can reach the level of existence which the Divine has created for men. In the Eastern religions the religious knowledge reveals the means whereby man can attain release from the inevitable Karma which now pursues him and thereby attain to a state where he is free from the limitations of existence which now ensnare him.

Religious beliefs in relation to the Divine and man are central because they present the intention and purpose which lie behind existence. They depict the abilities and inabilities which are the property of man, and which are the source both of his reliance upon himself and his despair with himself and his prospects. Man is the result of forces outside himself which are either divine in nature or part of the given characteristic of existence. None of the religions with which we have been concerned is content, however, to leave man in this situation. They exist in their respective fashions because in one manner or another they believe themselves to possess *the* Truth which reveals that man is not limited to that which he now experiences. Religion as we have been considering it inevitably leads to a presupposition regarding the fulfilment of man and it is at this point that religion has considered itself to be of most significance for man and his understanding of himself.

A. THE CHRISTIAN FAITH

Our discussion of Christian presuppositions has sought to make clear the beliefs which are the foundation upon which the Christian message concerning man's fulfilment rests. The Divine has revealed Himself to man in order to bring man into the intended and correct relationship with Him. The supreme and decisive event in which this revelation is to be found is the life, teachings, death, and resurrection of Jesus Christ. The conflicting beliefs in Christianity about the human and divine nature of Christ do not alter the fact of the general Christian emphasis upon Christ as the means whereby man is to receive his fulfilment. Orthodoxy has held in one form or another that by Christ's acceptance of death and his triumph over it, all those who accept him as their divine redeemer are freed from the finality of death and brought into a new relationship with God which will continue beyond this earthly life. The various deviations from the orthodox position have not altered this view in any marked degree. They may hold Christ to be no more than a divinely inspired man; they may place greater emphasis upon the responsibility of individual men to work for their own salvation, but in any case Jesus Christ is the supreme revelation of the divine plan for human fulfilment.

Since Christianity presupposes the soul or final essence of man to be of an immortal character, it follows that the condi-

tion or state of the soul will continue in some state of existence beyond this present life. Further, as this present existence
is one in which the Divine is of paramount importance, so also
will the Divine be a factor in the future. The Divine is not
limited to the world and the present, nor is man. The future
of man is as dependent upon God as is the present. In all
states of being man is a derivative creature receiving his existence and meaning from his relationship with his Creator.
Therefore, in his present life any consideration man gives
to his future must take the Divine into account, for it is only
in and through the Divine that human fulfilment is possible.

It is at this point that the Christian theory of the meaning
and place of human history is vitally important. Christianity
has held to the view that the world exists for a purpose and
not simply as a result of divine caprice. The world was
created by God and man placed in it by divine intent. Various
theories have been advanced as to the purpose behind God's
activity of creation. The main concern of the Christian faith
has been that divine purpose is here and man is a part of it.
As a part of the divine will and purpose man cannot, therefore,
consider his present life as but an interim experience with no
purpose or consequence.

Christian theories of history have usually agreed on the
point that God is acting in and through history. What happens
in the world may not be the result of God's action, for it may
have arisen as a result of the rebellion of man against God.
Nevertheless, the Divine is concerned with the event and seeks
to bring it and its results into relationship with His will.
Because of the limitations which the Divine has set upon Himself, this can only be done through the love and mercy which
God bestows upon man through Christ and the Holy Spirit.
God does not, in most contemporary Christian thought, seek
to coerce man into the right relationship with Him by bringing
about events of history which will turn man from his present
course of action. God is involved in history because He is in
intimate relationship with man who experiences history. He
is the Lord of History because He is able through His love and

grace to use history for the fulfilment of man and the accomplishment of His own purposes.

God acts in human history through the Holy Spirit. The Holy Spirit is the Divine present in the world of man making Himself known to man. Therefore, history may be considered to be both the product of God and of man. It is the result of man's activities in either case, but in one instance it is a reflection of the divine will and purpose through the influence of the Holy Spirit upon man, and in the other it is the product of man's activity apart from the Divine. One type is related to the Divine and is good because of the relationship, the other is apart from the Divine and is evil because of the separation. The former receives its value from its accord with the Divine will, while the latter is of disvalue because it arises from human self-concern which ignores the intimate relationship between God and man.

It is the Christian contention that man faces defeat in history when the relationship between God and man is not uppermost in man's mind. It is only when man is aware of his own self-defeating desires and purposes and turns to God that man's activities will bring about his own fulfilment in accord with the divine plan for man. When this occurs, man's activities are not in the final analysis his own, but are God's. Man is guided by the divine will because he is seeking in all that he does to fulfil that will. Man is no longer seeking to act on his own resources alone, but is aware that it is from God that he receives his strength and ability. Man is now living and acting in intimate relationship with the Divine; he is recognizing his derivative nature and finding resources which he did not know or possess heretofore. He is now living his life as the nature of his creation intended it to be lived.

Man is doomed to self-defeat when this relationship is broken. For Christianity the opportunity for the re-establishment of the connection between God and man was brought about by God in Jesus Christ. Man is offered salvation from has present state of rebellion and its consequences through an acceptance of God's forgiveness. Christ is the embodiment of the forgiving grace of the Divine. It is through him that it is brought to man, and it is by acknowledging his act that man accepts it. Such acknowledgment, however, constitutes more than a simple acceptance of Christ's activity as being a fact of history. In Christian conversion or dedication the individual man is acknowledging his dependence upon the Divine, his disobedient or sinful nature, his insufficiency, and that his own fulfilment is to be found only in relationship with God.

Christianity has held to different positions as to whether the grace of God confronting man through Jesus Christ is something which is resistible or irresistible. There is no doubt but what man does defy the Divine, but is that defiance the result of man's own decision or God's planning? Where freedom of the will has been denied, the divine grace has been held to be irresistible. All men are subject to God's omnipotence to the degree that they cannot resist His love if He desires them to accept it and, conversely, they cannot avail themselves of it if He in His wisdom has excluded them from it. However, theological constructions which have held to freedom of will in man have believed that man resists God's grace on his own account. The ability of free choice is given by God and the inclination to resist God results from the corrupt nature which man possesses as a result of his present condition of separation from God.

According to Christian thought the nature of history and of man's condition is such that even upon the re-establishment of the relationship between God and man in Jesus Christ the individual may not be said to have achieved or received total fulfilment. Human fulfilment is not limited to the present existence of man. The immortal soul of man is destined by God for something more than the present life and its experiences. This life and its experiences are of great significance for in them the relationship between God and man may be re-established and strengthened, but this is not the end. The purpose of life is that the relationship be strengthened once it has been re-established. It can only be strengthened by man's constant dedication and purposeful attempts to live up to all the relationship implies. It is for this reason that man lives and creates history, and it is only in the degree that man makes the relationship actual and dynamic that history works for the fulfilment of the divine purpose which, in actuality, is man's fulfilment.

Human fulfilment, then, is only possible in human life when man is reunited with God in Jesus Christ the recreator of the right relationship between God and man. It is at this point that Christianity enters into its most open conflict with the other religions of the world. In the next chapter we shall consider the views of the religions toward other religions and their values and shall note the degree of exclusiveness to the Christian claim that it is only in Jesus Christ that the relationship between man and God is brought into full flower. Christianity does not necessarily hold that other religious systems are of no value, but in most of its thought on the matter it has held them to be at least so inferior to the Christian message that if they are maintained in the face of the Christian claim, they are impediments to human fulfilment rather than aids.

We have noted that man does not conceive his fulfilment to be limited to his present earthly existence. There have been times and areas in history when such thought has existed. The major world religions which we are considering all look beyond the limitations of earthly existence and human history. Christianity has been interpreted throughout most of its history as being a religion whose primary message is one of immortality and the supra-earthly fulfilment of man. The various groups within Christianity today often place differing degrees of emphasis upon the importance of the condition and state of man after this life. None of them deny that such an existence is an essential Christian doctrine. The present mood of much of Christianity is to place emphasis, however, upon the necessity of the establishment of the proper relationship between man and God in this life. When this is done, then man has placed himself in the hands of the Divine. Since the Divine is a Being with purpose and has demonstrated His great love for man in His act of redemption in Jesus Christ, man's con-

cern need no longer be his own fulfilment now or in the
future, for that will flow automatically from God's love.

B. THE MUSLIM FAITH

The Muslim presupposition in regard to human fulfilment
shares with Christianity in the conviction that this fulfilment
is only to be found in a proper relationship to the Divine. In
both religions a denial of the relationship by man is not considered to dissolve its existence. Such a declaration on man's
part is the result of his own blindness to the reality of his
creaturehood; it impedes the relationship and its fruits, but
it does not establish man in any way as an independent being
without dependence upon the Divine. For Islam man's present
state and his future existence can only be considered in the
light of the divine will and purpose. All men are in relationship to the Divine whether they realize it or not. Their status
at any given time or place is determined by the divine will.
Their fulfilment is only to be found in the Divine, for their
existence itself is derived totally and completely from Allah.

We have seen that the Muslim theory concerning the nature
of man considers him to be completely incapable of any action
which is originated apart from the predetermination of Allah.
Man is predestined in all that he does. Therefore, human
fulfilment is also the result of divine action and will, and is
irresistible. If Allah determines that an individual is to be
saved, he will be saved. If the Divine determines that an
individual is not to attain fulfilment in some future state, he
will not. These matters are beyond human comprehension
and can only be accepted as further manifestations of Allah's
greatness and man's insignificance in comparison to Him.

As in Christianity, human fulfilment for Islam is identified
with the conception of salvation. By being a chosen one of
Allah, the individual is saved from the consequences of existence apart from Allah's grace and compassion. Such a separate existence is as wholly dependent upon Allah as any other,
but the consequences of it are death. If the Divine has selected
the individual to be saved from this consequence, such salva-

tion will result in the reception by the individual of the fulfilment decreed for him by Allah. Human fulfilment is in the hands of Allah and man receives or misses it according to His purpose, yet even in failing to receive it the individual is fulfilling the purposes of the sovereign Divine.

Salvation, for Islam, is a legalistic matter. Man is called upon to submit to Allah's will and power. The fact that he may not submit does not mean that he is not just as subject to that will as if he had submitted. In the one case he acknowledges it, and in the other he ignores or defies it. In either case, his action is determined by Allah, though the responsibility is his. Having submitted himself to Allah, the individual has gained a release from the death which awaits all creatures who are not destined by Allah for future existence. However, at this stage of submission the only assurance for the individual is that he will at some time be saved. The literature of Islam is vivid in its depiction of the nature of the life after earthly death which awaits all Muslims. The primary legalistic step is taken in the act of submission which assures man of ultimate salvation and fulfilment. Nevertheless, the degree of torment and of pleasure which awaits him in the future is determined by his actions in this life. Though he knows that if he is a true Muslim he will at some stage receive the pleasure which comes to man from Allah's bounty, it is possible that his lack of good deeds may greatly delay his entrance into the Paradise prepared for Muslims by Allah. At the time of the Day of Judgment, human deeds will be taken into account and even one who is destined by Allah for Paradise may find his entrance into it postponed.

For Islam, human history is the record of events which are predetermined by the Divine. The evil which man does, or which brings misfortune to man, is only evil from man's limited perspective and not from Allah's. All that is good in man's actions and in society is the result of Allah's foreordination. Human history is the record of Allah's power and sovereign will at work for His glorious purposes and is not to be judged by man.

There are those who will object to the emphasis we have put upon the legalistic and predetermined character of the Muslim conception of salvation. It is true that one can point to the sublime faith which motivates the pious Muslim. The Sufi mystics have produced some of the most stirring and beautiful religious literature, and have demonstrated that Islam has a place for human dedication and spiritual commitment in a degree equal to that of any religion. However, orthodox theological thought and its presuppositions are embedded in the conception of Allah as sovereign power to the degree that any consistent theology produced by Islam has been legalistic in character and has emphasized Allah's sovereignty while belittling man's worth and ultimate responsibility.

Human fulfilment in the present is to be found when man submits himself to the Divine and enters into the community of Islam. The individual is now a member of the Brotherhood of Believers and as such possesses a sign of the divine favor which is not given to those who are outside the Brotherhood. There can be no question but what the Muslim emphasis upon the community of the Faithful does bring well-being and meaning to the lives of those who are a part of it. Man does find fulfilment in meaningful relationships with his fellows, and for Islam this relationship is cemented by a common submission to the Divine which is the source and determiner of all life.

Human fulfilment in the future, like that in the present, is the result of submission to Allah. The individual is now assured of the protection and mercy of Allah which will result in an existence which fulfils all of man's dreams of pleasure and contentment. As a favored one of the Divine the fortunate individual will find fulfilment in the reflection of Allah's power and compassion which surrounds him. He is a creature of the Divine, and his ultimate destiny is to fulfil the purposes of the Divine. If he be one of those whose destiny it is to be chosen for Paradise, he shall find his fulfilment there; if not, his fulfilment is not to be experienced by himself, but even then his fateful destiny will fulfil the purposes of God.

C. THE HINDU FAITH

Hindu presuppositions concerning human fulfilment and the ultimate destiny of man also are derived from the fundamental theories which we have been discussing in the past chapters. The general position which is associated with the Upanishads as interpreted in Vedanta is the core around which most contemporary Hindu intellectual thought is clustered. In relation to human fulfilment or salvation (*moksha*) it expresses itself in what is known as *Jñāna Marga*. Along with this theory of human fulfilment there are two others of primary significance—*Karma Marga* and *Bhakti Marga*. (The word *Yoga* is sometimes used in place of *Marga*.) These three theories of salvation are the central streams of Hindu religious thought and practice which arise from the basic presuppositions concerning the nature of the Divine and the constitution of man.

Karma Marga may be said to be the continuation in modern Hinduism of religious thought which is connected with the earliest religious practices of India. In fact, it represents a strong current of religious thought and practice which is to be found in all religious systems around the world. It arises from the early conviction of man that he is dependent upon the Divine for his material sustenance and fulfilment in this life, and in future existences. Since this is so, it is necessary that he keep in good relationship with God or the gods, and this is to be done primarily through actions which please them. At the lower levels of all of the religions there is this current of thought and its resulting religious practice. At one level it means that the gods are to be appeased and their favor gained by offering them sacrifices which are pleasant to them. At another level it expresses itself in the conviction that man gains the favor of the Divine primarily by the doing of deeds which are demanded by the Divine. In Hinduism the latter is most important, although there is still present among large groups of the illiterate masses, religious belief and practice which are representative of the former.

For modern Hinduism, Karma Marga is the system or method whereby salvation can be obtained by good deeds. By good deeds is meant the following in one's life of the *Dharma* or divine law which is imperative upon the individual. This divine law is to be found primarily in the caste laws or duties which surround man, as well as in the ancient laws of living and behavior which are a part of Hindu society. By good actions one creates for himself a good Karma, and not a bad one. He is living in accord with, and not in opposition to, the divine law—the given. Human fulfilment in this view comes to man because he adjusts himself to the situation in which he has been placed by his deeds in past existences and by the divine will.

The differences in Hindu beliefs concerning the Divine, man, and existence are such that Karma Marga may be interpreted either as a system of its own or from the perspective of the upanishadic presuppositions which we have held to be the central fact of modern Hinduism. At the lower levels of Hindu religion the beliefs concerning existence beyond this one have little in common with the intellectual expressions which we have been describing. Where good actions are considered to be the primary method whereby man can establish right relationship with the deities it is believed that these deeds will bring about more prosperity in this life. This is the primary function of religion: the attainment of the good will and favor of the gods in order that life may be less disastrous and more pleasant. However, as we have indicated, man does not stop with consideration of his lot in this life alone. Right deeds in the station of life which is one's lot will bring about reward in the future. Since it is fundamental to Hinduism at all levels that actions produce their consequences, and these consequences cannot be escaped, it is believed that good actions in the present life will insure that the individual will find himself in a more favorable station of life in his next existence following rebirth. If he has gained extremely good favor in the sight of a particular deity he will spend a certain period between this present life and the next human existence in the realm or heaven of that deity. Here he will exist until his good deeds have been repaid before he returns to human existence. If he has completely failed to do good works he will either spend a period in punishment in a hell, or will return immediately to worldly existence at a level lower than his present one.

If Karma Marga is interpreted from the level of the philosophical-theological presuppositions of Vedanta it is held to be not the way to fulfilment or salvation for men, but simply a preliminary step in the process. The best that can be said for it is that it enables the individual to rise to a higher level of existence in which he will be able to progress further toward real fulfilment. At its worst it is a reflection of the confusion of man concerning the physical world and his actions in it. Man thinks that his deeds are of primary importance whereas, as we have seen, they are of a secondary and minor nature. However, taking modern Hinduism as a whole it must be said to be an integral part of Hinduism's thought and practice. The strength of caste lies in the concern with actions and their part in gaining the approval of the Divine. The Upanishads, the Laws of Manu, the Bhagavad Gita, and many other religious writings point to the importance of the individual's fulfilling his own *Dharma* or lot in life. Man exists under the imperative to do what is required of him by the divine order of things. If he does not do so, he will suffer.

Bhakti Marga is much more closely associated with the fundamental presuppositions of philosophical-theological Hinduism than is Karma Marga. Its emphasis is upon love or devotion to the Divine—the *Bhagavat*. The two largest groups of modern Hinduism, the Vaisnava and the Śaiva, are reflections of Bhakti thought as it has developed over the centuries. Bhakti has often been the subject of comparison with Christianity, and has become a general term used to describe aspects in Hinduism and Buddhism which reflect emphasis upon the relationship between the Divine and man as being one of divine grace and human adoration.

For Bhakti, the Divine is to be known primarily through the various incarnations (*avataras*) of God which have appeared in the world. The Divine is to be adored by man as the source of man and of all existence. Any one of the many incarnations may be the object of this adoration, and the differences between the various Bhakti groups often arise out of their emphasis upon one of the avataras to the neglect of others. However, each of the avataras must be seen as being incarnations of the one God. The Divine has made Himself known to men through entering into the world at various times in order to relieve man from sin. It is in the form of the avataras that He is known to man and worshipped by man.

Bhakti Marga agrees with the presuppositions concerning man which we have described in that it holds that all souls issue forth from the Divine. It differs mainly in its insistence that these souls after their separation from God exist as separate distinct entities throughout eternity. Man, then, is primarily a soul which is divine in its origin and its subsequent nature because it has emerged from the Divine. This soul is chained to birth and rebirth until by the means of adoration of its divine source it is able to return to the Divine where it exists eternally. However, it is important to note that it is not absorbed into the Divine from whence it came, but exists as a separate entity which can be distinguished from the Divine.

An important feature of Bhakti is that while it is necessary for man to adore the Divine in order to obtain fulfilment and to return to his divine source, the element of divine grace is of primary significance. Karma or deeds are important in that they will be repaid in some existence beyond this one, but they do not release man from the round of rebirths. Ultimate salvation or fulfilment for the soul is only obtained as a result of the grace, the loving compassion of the Adorable Bhagavat— the Divine. Good works are only really good if they are done disinterestedly out of the adoration and dedication one feels toward the Divine. But no work, however good, is sufficient to release the soul from its involvement in worldly existence; this is only achieved when the Divine enters into the heart of those who adore Him.

Bhakti Marga may be considered as one of the three primary methods for the attainment of salvation which is an integral part of Hinduism. It does not place the emphasis upon good works which Karma Marga does, though it is concerned with them. Its primary presupposition is that love is paramount in the nature of the Divine. The divine source from which man and all existence come enables those who turn to Him in adoration to obtain fulfilment through the operation of His grace. That fulfilment is achieved when the individual soul returns to its source where it exists forever in a state of bliss serving the Adorable.

Jñāna Marga is the direct result of the fundamental presuppositions concerning Religious Knowledge, the Divine, and Man which we have presented as the common core around which the major variations of Hinduism are clustered. In varying degree the major groups of modern Hinduism reflect the thought which we have termed Vedanta. Jñāna Marga reflects Vedanta in its highest and most refined form. Whereas Karma and Bhakti Marga are the ways to fulfilment by works and by adoration, Jñāna Marga is the way to fulfilment by knowledge. It must be indicated at the very start that by "knowledge" it is not meant that man can gain salvation through the use of his rational faculties. This "knowledge" is intuitive; it is that awareness or cognition which comes suddenly when the individual through reflection and meditation comes to know the Truth. It is the expression of religious mysticism wherein the individual comes to recognize his identity with the Divine and the fact that in his ultimate essence he is not an individual.

In all of its many variations today Hinduism is agreed that fulfilment for mankind lies beyond the sphere of earthly existence. In fact, it is existence itself which curbs man and keeps him away from fulfilment. Salvation for Hinduism consists in escape from the world. Existence in the sphere of time and space is the curse which binds man to the continual round of birth and rebirth. In each life he experiences, man is forced to commit more actions, and each action involves him still further in the very process he wishes to escape. Every deed must have its recompense with the consequence that the true "self" within man is more enmeshed in the world of māyā. The "self" is dimly aware of its own true stature, and seeks to escape from its involvement in the world of secondary reality with its constant change and flux and lack of Reality. This world of movement and change (*samsāra*) has ensnared the "self" to the extent that the "self" has lost its true self-consciousness with the result that it engages in actions which further its imprisonment.

Our discussion of the general presuppositions of Hinduism as revealed in Hindu philosophical-theological speculation has indicated that the inmost essence of man is conceived as being identified with the Divine. Vedanta thought, therefore, has held salvation to be the release of the "self" from that which misleads it into not being aware of its identity with the divine Self. Emancipation from rebirth lies in that state of infiniteness that a man attains when he knows his own "self" for what it is—Divine. This is true knowledge; it is Jñāna. Vedanta maintains that without this knowledge all deeds are of no avail in gaining for man the full emancipation and fulfilment which is rightfully his destiny. Karma Marga and Bhakti Marga are but further examples of the soul's misunderstanding of itself and its true nature. The endless course of transmigration is for the ignorant, and even their best attempts to escape it do not bring what they truly seek. It is the wise man who has divested himself of all desires and attachments to māyā—the man who by intuitive knowledge knows himself to be Brahman, and who in the very fact of that knowledge is released from existence and the causal chain of deeds. As one of the Upanishads puts it:

The knot of the heart is loosened,
All doubts are cut off,

And one's deeds cease
When He [Brahman] is seen—both the higher and the
lower.

Knowledge of the "self" reveals that all man's passions, all his limitations of experience, all that is evil in him, all that is transient and finite in him—is false. The individual who knows the "self" does not know but, rather, is "pure knowledge" himself. If man knows the "self" he is not limited by anything, for he is the infinite; he does not suffer death, for he is immortal. It is important to notice that Jñāna emphasizes that emancipation or release from the bonds of existence is not a new acquisition, nor is it the product, or effect, or result of any action. It always exists as the Truth of man's nature. Man is always emancipated and free though he does not seem to be so, and appears to suffer rebirth and the troubles which are a consequence of it. But, this is illusion (māyā) which arises from man's ignorance of the true nature of his "self."

Again, true knowledge of the "self" does not lead to emancipation; it is emancipation and, therefore, fulfilment. All limitations and sufferings are true only so long as man does not know the "self." Hence, emancipation is the natural and only goal of man simply because it represents the real nature and essence of man. So long as the "self" identifies itself with its desires, it wills and acts according to them, and reaps the fruits of its deeds in the present and in future lives. It is only when the individual comes to know the highest Truth about himself, that he is *the* essence and principle of the universe, the immortal and the infinite, that he ceases to have desires, and turning away from them realizes the ultimate destiny which has been kept from him by his own ignorance. So long as man keeps himself involved in the world by his attachments to it, and actions in it, he suffers pleasures and pains, disease and death, in a never ending cycle.

When man retires from all attachments which surround him and enters into his true unchangeable being, he is in a state where there is no change and no movement. Here there is no difference between objects because no such categories as subject and object are operative as all that is, is subject. Man has reached fulfilment, for he has cut himself off from the causal chain of Karma which has bound him to existence. He has entered into the state of absolute infinitude or pure intelligence, pure being, and pure blessedness.

Modern Hinduism may be said to be a composite of the three conceptions of salvation and human destiny which we have been discussing. While those Hindus who are members of a group which is primarily Bhakti in nature will place their emphasis on Bhakti as the proper and only means of salvation, yet they will have a place for the thought of both Karma and Jñāna Marga. Each of the groups will differ with the others in particulars, and often over fundamental points, but they are bound together by the presuppositions which they share in common. They are convinced that man's fulfilment lies beyond the illusory world which hides the Divine from man and ensnares man in its causal chain. They seek to aid man to achieve his true destiny by presenting to him the methods whereby he can rise above his present lot.

D. THE BUDDHIST FAITH

The theories of Buddhism concerning human fulfilment have been foreshadowed to a large extent by our previous discussions of the presuppositions of Buddhism as well as by our examination of Hindu beliefs regarding salvation. Transmigration and Karma are basic doctrines of all Buddhist thought and are the most real factors which must be faced by man as he surveys his situation. The two doctrines combine in Buddhism, as in Hinduism, to create an almost automatic principle to explain the human predicament and its continuation. Karma, with its cause and effect relationship to the situation of man, determines the form which transmigration will take. Transmigration explains the method by which Karma operates, while Karma accounts for the cause or necessity for Transmigration. Each complements the other.

Buddhism reflects Hindu Karma Marga in the popular

religion of the masses. Actions determine the state of existence in the next birth. The individual is called upon to live according to the precepts of the Buddha for laymen in order that he may escape one of the many hells to which bad Karma may take man. It is popularly believed that exceptionally good Karma will result in a period of reward in a heaven of some deity before return to earthly existence. This is present in both Theravadin and Mahayana.

Bhakti Marga is present also in both the major groups of Buddhism. The popular religion of the Southern Buddhist countries is to all intents and purposes the same as popular Bhakti in Hinduism, while much of Mahayana reflects the Bhakti emphasis on love and adoration for deity which is to be found in all the major religions of the world. By adoration of some deity in the popular pantheon man receives the special care and blessings of the god. By the faithful performance of worship rites the individual establishes a special relationship between himself and the god, and he will be rewarded in the future by existence in the heaven or paradise of the god. As a result both Theravadin and Mahayana Buddhism on their popular levels have developed a great number of heavens and hells to which man may go in interim periods between his various existences on earth. In Mahayana these supraearthly states are more a reflection of the theological schools of thought than in Southern Buddhism where they are in opposition to the official doctrines as expounded by the more orthodox monastic orders. In one they are representative of theological thought which is more attuned to the basic religious desires of the people; while in the other they exist because of these popular spiritual desires, but in contradiction to the presuppositions of the religious leadership.

The fundamental theories of Theravadin Buddhism regarding man and his fulfilment arise from the same general beliefs present in Hinduism. Placing special emphasis upon cause and effect, it holds man to be bound to earthly existence by his actions. Earthly existence involves suffering and misery. Man is bound to this because his desires lead him to actions, with the inevitable result that man in some form must experience the effects of the actions. Man finds himself in the sphere of pain and conflict, and any action he undertakes only binds him more firmly to repeated unpleasant experience. Fulfilment, therefore, is only to be found when man is able to escape from such a miserable state. Popularly this has meant that the protection and aid of the gods in their various forms must be gained, while the theoretical presuppositions of the religion have placed emphasis upon the ultimate dependence of man upon himself.

Theravadin Buddhism has placed its emphasis upon the "Middle Path" presented by the Buddha. By strict dedication to the teachings of the Buddha man can overcome the chains which bind him to existence. He is not to follow either the extremes of self-indulgence, or of asceticism. The eight precepts of the "Middle Path" will lead man to the point where craving or desire is extinguished, and when this is done, man will cease to be and will pass into the state of Nibbāna. Fulfilment, then, lies in the attainment of Nibbāna—a state which cannot be described nor adequately understood by man because it is a realm beyond the comprehension of man. Human categories and concepts do not apply to Nibbāna; that which is infinite and unlimited cannot be described in finite and limited terms.

Mahayana Buddhism is a mixture of the two levels we have just referred to in Theravadin Buddhism. If one should study only one of the more esoteric sects of Mahayana he would find that much of the thought is a reflection of the intellectual level of Theravadin. If one should limit his knowledge only to one of the more popular sects of Mahayana he would find that it was much more closely connected in thought and practice with its counterparts in the popular religion of Southern Buddhism. Both groups contain within themselves the various aspects of religious thought and practice which are common to much of religion around the world.

The various sects or denominations of Mahayana, however, have been more sensitive to the religious thought and needs

of the average man than has Theravadin. Mahayana has incorporated what might be termed Karma Marga and Bhakti
Marga into its basic presuppositions on the basis of its belief
that it represents the highest and final revelations of the
Buddha. At its profound levels it places emphasis upon
thought which is of the nature of Jñāna Marga, and by the
combination of the three aspects of religion it possesses an
appeal to almost any level of religious inclination.

The decisive difference between the two major branches
of Buddhism in regard to the fulfilment or salvation of man
lies in the Mahayana emphasis upon the role of saviors (Bodhisattvas) in aiding man to rise above his present limitations.
Most Mahayana conceptions of the Bodhisattvas and their
functions place stress upon adoration of them by man. Bhakti
is primary in the great majority of the popular Mahayana
sects. Karma Marga or right action is coupled with Bhakti
in that adoration of the Bodhisattva consists in certain pre-
scribed actions which give evidence of the individual's devotion. Ethical demands are also made upon the individual if
he is to rise to the state where he will be freed from his present limitations and himself enter into the way of Bodhisattvahood. No religion of vital consequence to human life is able
to restrict itself purely to the realm of thought and to exclude
action. Mahayana has emphasized the importance of inner
thought and devotion, but in its best moments it has also
clearly discerned the importance of calling its adherents to
actions and modes of behavior which rise above the usual
animal appetites and self-concern of man.

The various systems of theology within Mahayana look
upon salvation as consisting in escape from the sufferings of
existence, but they conceive of it as being related also to an
activity which both aids one's own fulfilment and that of
others. The salvation which comes in experiencing any one
of the many heavens of the various Buddhas or Bodhisattvas
is only a relative matter. It is a much higher state of existence
than the present one, but it is not fulfilment. The true and final
destiny of man is the attainment of Nirvāna. In most Maha-

yana systems this involves much which we have noted in the three paths of Hindu attainment, but with the addition of the conception of the "Way of the Bodhisattva." The individual is invited to embark on the path to Bodhisattvahood himself by taking the vows of a Bodhisattva "to be." He is thus dedicating himself to the service and aid of his fellow beings while he is working for his own fulfilment. A Bodhisattva, who is a "Buddha to be," is one who has approached to the threshold of Nirvāna but has refrained from entering into it in order that he may lead others to it. A Buddhist in this life who has taken the Bodhisattva vows is one who has set out to live the type of life which will both bring him to the higher Bodhisattva state, and aid others in advancing further along the path to Enlightenment or fulfilment. His own fulfilment is thus involved with the fulfilment of others.

One of the most difficult aspects of the theories of both Hinduism and Buddhism in regard to salvation arises from their insistence upon the nature of Nirvāna or Nibbāna. Westerners have been all too willing to assume that by the use of terms which have been translated into Western languages as "nothingness," "non-existence," and so forth, it was meant that the final destiny of man is without content or meaning. It must be realized that it is only the more subtle and intellectual formulations of the two religions which have used such terms. And more important, these terms have been used to convey the firm conviction that existence in such a state is completely different from anything which can be conceived by man. If life in the world is "existence," then Nirvāna is "non-existence." If we now are, if we have "being," the ultimate destiny awaiting man is of such a different character that it cannot be said that man will "have being"; he will be in a state of "non-being." The words, terms, symbols, concepts, and categories that man must use even to discuss Nirvāna are misleading and must not be taken as more than indications, and even these indications must be denied. Life as it is understood must be negated for it involves entanglement and struggle. Nirvāna is the opposite and can only be described negatively. It is true that both of the religions do give positive terms to their references to Nirvāna. In so doing they are indebted to terms used in their scriptures and the reports which have been given to them by those who are believed to have experienced Nirvāna in some form while in this life. Nirvāna may be termed "bliss" or "Enlightenment," but even these terms must be recognized as being completely inadequate.

The Western religions have also used such terms and insisted upon the inadequacy of human language. This has been true particularly in their mystical expressions wherein the individual mystic has been so filled with consciousness of the Divine that he has been able to describe his experience only in the most esoteric and fanciful fashion. What he has experienced is too great for the human mind to grasp; it is so totally different from what man knows in this earthly sphere that finite language fails to convey it. The sphere of Eternity cannot be limited to, nor defined in, the sphere of Time.

V. WESTERN AND EASTERN THEORIES OF RECONCILIATION

There are many today who look to religion for the solution to the world's problems. What they conceive the solution to be is determined to a large extent by the religion of which they are a part. Those for whom religion is a vital element of life have discovered that religion brings meaning to their individual and social problems on the immediate personal level. Life is rich because of their Faith; it is bearable because of the assurances religion brings them, and for many it is challenging because their religious beliefs confront them demandingly. It gives them a picture of an ideal for man here on earth in his present existence, as well as bestowing a conception of the unity of man in his common humanity and relationship to the source of his being. This is true even in a religion such as Buddhism, which in one of its major expressions denies an Ultimate Source, or God. As we have seen, in Southern Buddhism life is somehow a related thing in which all men share; men are the products of a common process and they are to seek for a common end.

If this is true for religious man, does it not follow that he should seek to share this which is of value to him with those who do not possess it? If religion has brought meaning to individual life, and a basis for close and high relationship between peoples on a limited regional scale, should it not be expected that the world and its large problems would benefit by the universal application of religion in the present crisis? The answer is obviously yes, and the attempts to bring religion to bear on the manifold issues which confront mankind have been many. To a large degree these attempts have taken place within the local regional areas of a particular religion. Each religion has had its thinkers, its reformers, its leaders, who have sought to apply the fundamental insights and demands of the faith to the problems of the people and society who are its responsibility.

All religions have not participated to a like degree in the effort to bring their separate messages to the attention of the world. Three of the religions we have been discussing—Christianity, Islam, and Buddhism—have considered themselves throughout their history to be universal. Each has endeavored by separate means to bring new peoples under its influence, and each has succeeded in spreading to areas far from the place of its origin. The other religion, Hinduism, has limited itself to appealing to the peoples within its immediate geographic locale, but its influence has spread far beyond its borders.

In the present era of the world's history, none of these religions can be considered to be limited in its scope or regional in its nature. The traditional universal religions are now challenged by all areas of the world—areas which are no longer separated by insurmountable distances and totally unknown peoples. The fourth religion, Hinduism, is rapidly changing from its traditional provincialism and claiming for itself a universal validity which is fully equal to that maintained by the others. Each of the religions is now committed to a theory or conviction of its own universal nature which brings it into direct conflict with the claims of the others. Each is becoming cognizant of the fact that the century which lies ahead of necessity will be a time of claims and counter-claims in which it must take part or perish.

At some time in the history of each of the religions they have been engaged in conflict with other religions in order to bring their message to bear upon greater numbers of people. In their periods of greatest inner strength that vitality has expressed itself in expansionist activities; in periods of lethargy missionary activity has been forgotten or curtailed. The nature of the expansion of these religions has varied greatly. In some instances it has been by the preaching and sharing of the belief, in others it has been by military activity and the establishment of larger political units, and in others it has been by the slow spreading of a culture through the course of centuries. These variations are not to be identified individually with one of the religions and excluded from the history of the others, nor are they to be considered as no longer in operation. Hinduism is still engaged in bringing the diverse peoples of the Indian subcontinent into itself; Buddhism continues to penetrate into the primitive areas of the Pacific and East Asia; Islam is actively engaged in spreading the message of the Prophet in Central Africa; and Christianity is expressing its missionary passion on a world-wide scale. In the case of each, peaceful sharing, political power and activity, and cultural penetration are in operation.

In the course of this activity, and in conjunction with the theological development of the religion, theories have arisen as to the relationship of the individual religion with other religions which it meets. These theories have been based upon the presuppositions with which we were concerned in the previous chapters, particularly upon the belief held as to religious knowledge, or the nature of the revelation upon which the religion is founded. It is not true that in all instances these views of one religion toward another religion, or all other religions, were deliberately thought-out plans of action arrived at after careful consideration of the theological and practical matters involved. None of the religions has approached the problem of its relationships with other religions with the thought that it might possibly give up its own position in favor of the other, nor has any one of them sought to engage in a comparison of its thought with that of another in a deliberately objective fashion which it was believed could conceivably result in the adoption of the other position. The theories of relationship between a religion and other religions have arisen from the certainty that the religion with which one starts is superior, and for the average member of the

religion this has been a matter of dogmatic belief. Where the
theories have been theologically and intellectually grounded
they have arisen from the basic presuppositions of the faith
and have not, therefore, succeeded in establishing themselves
on a rational basis acceptable to men of all religions.

Religion has not been, and cannot be, purely a matter of
intellectual assent. Therefore, it must be realized that in
the relationships and conflicts of the religions in the coming
decades the religious allegiances of mankind are not going to
be determined simply by the intellectual acceptability or
rational coherence of a religion. The spirit of the present age
will demand that these shall play their part, but the nature of
religion will thwart any attempts to make religion only, or
fundamentally, a body of thought rationally defensible and
intellectually acceptable.

To avoid a repetitious discussion of the positions of each
of the religions, and to make more clear the basic views
which the religions of today have toward each other, we shall
not treat each of the religions separately. The predominant
theories concerning the attitudes of the different religions
toward each other can best be discerned by treating the major
theories as they are expressed in the religions in which they
are found, rather than by a systematic listing and discussion
of all theories which have appeared in each religion. The religions which have been engaging our attention have not
exhibited a uniform amount of concern with the problem of
inter-religious relationships in the past, and one of them has
so far shown little concern in the present.

1. The Religions of the West

The two "universal" religions which are shaped in part by
the Semitic heritage of religious exclusiveness which they
share, Christianity and Islam, have demonstrated throughout
their history an intolerance of other religious views. While a
detailed investigation of their separate histories will indicate
that there have been periods and areas in which they have

allowed other religious groups to exist within their midst, their basic religious beliefs, and the resulting nature of the two religions as they have developed, have resulted in a strongly negative attitude toward all foreign religions.

The conception of the nature of revelation which is common to both religions is not one which allows the possibility of the existence of equally valid revelations. When an individual or a group has refused to accept the validity of the revelation upon which either of the two religions rests, then in the eyes of the members of the religion, they have declared themselves to be in opposition to God. In earlier periods of history such opposition was often met with violent physical force of which neither religion is proud today. The idea of broad toleration in religion has not been characteristic in the West in the past, nor is it yet in all areas.

Contemporary theories concerning the relationship between religions are not necessarily new theories. In Christian thought in this matter some of the earliest theologians, including the Apostle Paul, presented what they considered to be the Christian attitude toward non-Christian religions. We find strains of thought wherein the other religions were considered to be creations of Satan, as well as arguments that Christianity is the completion and "crown" of the other religions, or at least of some of them. These and similar theories have existed down to the present with variations of the first theory being the most accepted during the greater part of Christian history.

Christianity was brought face to face with the problem in the modern period due to its embarkation upon the great campaign of foreign missions in the nineteenth century. The advance of Western civilization and technology into the non-Western world, which has been an outstanding feature of the last two centuries, was accompanied by a corresponding outreach of Christianity in the form of active campaigns to bring the Christian gospel to all men. Western imperialism, colonialism, and economic trade were supplemented by the Christian religion.

Three general attitudes have shown themselves during these

centuries in which Christianity has been in constant contact with the other religions of the world. Each of them has had its spokesmen, two of them have had and continue to have influence among a great many Christian people, and each of the three has proved to be inadequate to meet the problems brought about by the encounter of Christianity with the world's religions. They are the ways of Radical Displacement, Syncretism, and Fulfilment.

The theory of Radical Displacement is a view which would be expected from a religion which holds itself to be the possessor of the unique revelation of God to man. It says, in effect, that since we possess *the* religious knowledge which is available to man it is incumbent upon all others to give up the beliefs they now hold and accept those which have been given by God. Once the basic presupposition upon which Christianity rests is granted, it would seem to be logical to accept the theory of Radical Displacement.

In practice this theory has been the modern missionary expression of the traditional Christian opposition to all other religions. In the mission field this has meant an uncompromising attitude on the part of Christians toward the religions which surround them. The Christian message has been presented with the demand that those of other religions leave their present religious faiths and reject them entirely in favor of Christianity. Where the missionary has been thoroughgoing in his following of the theory, particularly in dealing with primitive religions, he has sought at all costs to wipe out any vestiges of the non-Christian beliefs.

The theory of Syncretism in the relationship between religions has a long history. Early in the history of religions we have record of those who have set out to take the best from the different religions and sought to combine these beliefs into one universal religion. All such attempts have failed to recognize, however, that a religion is a unified body of belief and practice. It is extremely difficult, if not impossible, to take one item from a religion, to separate it from the presuppositions upon which it rests, and to incorporate it into a hybrid system of religious beliefs which do not share those presuppositions and the individual history of development which it has experienced.

In Christian history Syncretism as a method for the reconciliation of non-Christian religions with Christianity has been more covert than overt. There have been few who have been considered Christian in the orthodox sense who have advocated such a program. This does not alter the fact, however, that Christianity has incorporated the thought of other religions into its own system of belief and practice. The early centuries of Christianity are filled with the absorption and syncretism of aspects of religious thought and practice of the Greco-Roman world into Christianity; certain of these beliefs and acts have become an accepted part of modern Christianity. During the centuries the local indigenous religions of many areas which are now Christian have become part of Christianity in those regions.

In the modern period syncretism has had advocates only in a very limited sense, and a more adequately descriptive term is "adaptation." There have been instances wherein some particular feature of a non-Christian religion has appeared to certain Christians to be worthy of incorporation into Christianity in the area where the religion is in existence. They have discovered that this belief or religious practice is not, so they thought, in opposition to the beliefs and spirit of Christianity, and have held that its adoption by Christianity would strengthen the appeal of Christianity to the people of the non-Christian religion. Syncretism in this sense is not so much the attempt to take the best from other religions and incorporate them into Christianity, as it is the attempt to allow the presence in Christianity of features in other religions which are not in opposition to the Christian message, nor to the living of the Christian life by those who might hold to the belief.

However, here again the problem of the close interrelationship between any one aspect of a religion and all other features of the religion must be taken into account. If it is held that there is nothing anti-Christian in some feature of a non-Christian religion, will those who have had the belief before they became Christians be able to hold the belief in a Christian context without also maintaining the non-Christian presuppositions which supported the belief originally? It generally has been the conviction of Christian scholars and missionaries that the dangers of syncretism and adaptation are so great that it can be allowed only in the most isolated cases, if at all.

The theory of Fulfilment has often been referred to as the conception of Christianity as the "Crown" of the other religions. This is an outgrowth of the belief that Christianity furnishes the answers to the religious longings of humanity around the world, and in so doing it serves as the capstone to the religious insights which are present in the other religions. Where these religions are in error it sets them right, and where they were on the right path it takes them to the goal toward which they were seeking and working. The religions of mankind are "fulfilled" by the supreme revelation of the Divine given in Jesus Christ, and by accepting this revelation they are demonstrating the sincerity which has motivated them in their attempts to know God.

This approach to the problem of the relationship between religions was very popular in the last decades of the nineteenth and early decades of the twentieth century. There were many Christian missionaries, scholars, and laymen who felt that such a position was justified on the basis of the values they found in the non-Christian religions. They were convinced that such a policy or theory incorporated into missionary activity demonstrated Christian love and admiration for the sincere religious longings and accomplishments of those who had not had the benefit of the revelation in Christ.

The problem, however, is that it is hardly correct to call Christianity the crown of Hinduism, for example, when the presuppositions of the two religions are so extremely different. Where one religion holds to a belief that there have been many incarnations of God, it is difficult to conceive of a religion which completely denies this as being the fulfilment of the first. Where the one religion is committed to the presupposition that man is tied to a series of purposeless existences by a causal chain which is burdensome, and the other religion firmly maintains that man has but one earthly life and that it is an opportunity for joyous development as a child of God, it would appear to be extremely unlikely that the latter is a logical fulfilment of the former. The knowledge we now possess of the non-Christian religions would seem to forbid any easy assumptions of fulfilment on the part of intelligent Christian thinkers.

It will be observed immediately that these three attitudes toward the other religions all proceed from the assumption that Christianity is the true and universal religion. In one instance, the other religions are to cease to exist; in the second, only their best and valid features are to be preserved; and in the last, they are to recognize that what they now possess are at best only beginnings toward the Truth to be found in Christianity. These arguments may be justified and understandable from the Christian point of view, but it takes little understanding of man and of the other religions to recognize that these theories have not been and will not be enthusiastically received by non-Christians.

As would be expected, Radical Displacement has received the most bitter denunciation from non-Christians. On the surface it would appear to deny any validity to the non-Christian religions, declaring them to be so far below Christianity as to be, in reality, of no worth whatsoever. A word of defense of the theory needs to be made at this point. The modern proponent of Radical Displacement is often an individual who possesses great knowledge of the other religions. Because of this knowledge he is aware that admirable qualities are to be found in these religions. In many cases he has had the privilege of knowing adherents to them who have demonstrated great qualities of spiritual insight and living. Such a Christian, therefore, in reality is not saying that there is no value in these religions, but is declaring his Christian conviction that these values fade into insignificance when seen in the light of the revelation in Jesus Christ. There is, he maintains, no reason why even these values should not be discarded in favor of the much greater values which will become available with the adoption of Christianity.

Again, the modern proponents of Radical Displacement are aware of the necessity of using the indigenous culture and ethos of the non-Christian religions in the spreading of the Christian message. At this point they differ greatly from many earlier exponents of the theory. They realize that Christianity cannot be expected to express itself in the same forms in the different cultures of the world. However, they are caught in the difficulty of determining to what degree the culture and ethos of a non-Christian area is bound to the religion with which it has been associated historically. Fearful lest the Christian revelation be adulterated by its contact with foreign religious thought, they have tended to advocate a missionary program which inevitably leads to a radical uprooting of the Christian convert from his cultural heritage and indigenous society.

With the present trend toward a more conservative Christian theology in many areas, Radical Displacement has received a new impetus in the last years. The reaffirmation of the radical and discontinuous nature of the Christian revelation has meant that the other religions are conceived to be greatly inferior to the Gospel. The result has been an even greater growth of an impression of arrogance on the part of Christians in the minds of non-Christians which has resulted in a widening of the gulf between the religions. The defense of the Christian upholders of the completely different and superior nature of the Christian revelation, namely, that they are merely human and imperfect messengers of God's self-revelation, has not removed the sting from the Christian claim. But, of course, the most important fact is that the non-Christian has not been able to see the fundamental claim that the revelation in Jesus Christ is uniquely superior to his own religious knowledge.

A further theory of the relationship between the religions,

one which has not been characteristic of the Christian attitude and which is accepted by very few Christians, was put forward a few years ago by Professor William E. Hocking, an eminent philosopher and Christian leader. Suggesting the method of what he called "Reconception," Professor Hocking argued that these next years should be devoted to a co-operative study by all of the religions of their fundamentals. In the course of such a study he expressed the hope that they would jointly come to a greater realization of the individual essence of each of the religions. Further, he suggested, that the co-operative effort of the task would bring greater understanding between the participants as well as enabling them to discover the common nature of the religious experience and insights upon which their religions are founded. Reconception would not overlook the values in other religions which is the great danger of Radical Displacement, nor would it create a hybrid religion of no inner structure and integrity as would the method of Syncretism.

Reconception may be characterized as an expansion of the technique of Fulfilment in that it does hold that there are those factors in the non-Christian religions which are of value to the Christian and to the non-Christian. It conceives of the great religions of the world serving as means for the fulfilment of each other. Co-operatively they shall instruct, challenge, inspire, and aid each other as they set out in the task of "re-conceiving" themselves and the presuppositions upon which they rest. By this mutual process the horizons of each will be lifted, including Christianity, to the extent that the religious knowledge which has been given to man will be more correctly and fully understood and applied.

Those who possess even an elementary knowledge of Islam will recognize that by its very nature it has not been given to the development of elaborate theories concerning the relationships between religions. Even in the modern day there has been little mention by Muslim scholars of this problem. This arises from the fact that the fundamental presupposition of Islam that the revelation given to Muhammad and recorded in the Koran is unique and final, has inevitably led to an intolerance of other religions which has expressed itself in Radical Displacement.

However, it is not sufficient to stop with this brief characterization. The recognition of the presence of value in the "religions of the book" by Muhammad gives indication that when Islam does come to reassess its position, it has a resource which may be useful to it in the development of a new attitude toward at least some of the non-Muslim religions. Of the religions with which we have been concerned as leading participants in the world religious scene today, Christianity is the only religion which fits into the original category as it was conceived by Muhammad. Though orthodox Islam shows little inclination at the present time to enter into relationship with non-Muslim religions, if it should ever do so, it has a koranic basis for understanding with Christianity. In the past in separate instances it has shown inclination to do so and it can only be hoped that it will do so again.

Both Syncretism and Fulfilment have had their place in Islamic history, though in general these have been the result of practical circumstance rather than official theology. Indigenous pre-Muslim religious thought and practice are to be found in many areas of Islam as an integral part of the religious lives of loyal Muslims. Shia Islam, in particular, evidences the influence of pre-Muslim religious thought in the areas where it has flourished, while Sunni Islam has not been as strict in its insistence upon the "pure" Faith as it might be thought. The important thing is that once the major presuppositions of Islam have been adopted by converts, Islam has not been of a puritan nature in any consistent fashion.

We are confronted today, therefore, with an attitude on the part of the religions of the West which cannot be said to be one of a conciliatory nature. As we have indicated repeatedly, this is largely the result of the firm belief of each of the religions that they are the recipients, declarers, and custodians of *the* revealed Word of God to man. While it is possible for them in particular instances to co-operate with other religions

for immediate objectives, it is not possible for them to ignore
their fundamental claims of superiority. As we have suggested, the fact that they do not claim this superiority as being
a result of attainment on their part, but rather as a gift of the
Divine, does not ease the assertion in the minds of members
of the other religions. It remains to be seen as to what effect
the more conciliatory thought of the urbanized lay Muslim
will have upon Islamic thought in the coming years. It is
also to be wondered as to whether the "humanism" now present in the Christian areas, and which is influential among
many Christian laymen, will modify the exclusive stand which
Christianity has generally taken.

2. The Religions of the East

In the view which they have toward other religions, the
two leading religions of the East, Hinduism and Buddhism,
reflect a greatly different attitude from that of Christianity
and Islam. Buddhism as a product of the early Hindu religious ethos has not developed a theory in the matter which
has differed to any appreciable degree from the traditional
Indian or Hindu attitude. In fact, Buddhism has expressed
what may properly be called the modern Hindu view more
than Hinduism itself has done. By its evangelistic expansion
into far wider areas it has had the necessity and opportunity
to demonstrate the Eastern attitude of tolerance in a larger
measure than Hinduism, which has confined itself to a more
limited area. We may, therefore, discuss the theory of the
relationship between religions to be found in the East as a
common possession of both the leading Eastern religions.
However, it does need to be said that in the present era
Hinduism has been a more dynamic exponent of the theory,
although traditionally it has not considered itself to be uni-
versalistic as has Buddhism.

Modern scholarship has devoted a great amount of attention to the question as to what degree Buddhism may properly
be termed an expression of Hinduism, rather than a com-

pletely independent religion in its own right. Some Hindu scholars have given long arguments seeking to demonstrate that ideal Buddhism in a large degree is ideal Hinduism. Certain Buddhist scholars, and non-Buddhist scholars, have insisted that such is not the case. While this problem is beyond the scope of our discussion, yet it must be mentioned in order that we may be fully conscious of the close relationship between the two religions. The founder of Buddhism came from the background of Hinduism, he began his religious life and search in an approved Hindu manner, and in declaring his teachings he was dependent upon Hindu thought and expressions. After his death Buddhism spent its formative years in the midst of Hinduism and could not escape the influence of the Hindu religious spirit of which it was a product. No matter what position may be taken in the scholarly argument concerning the relationship between the two religions, all are forced to recognize the interrelationship between them.

From the standpoint of our concern this is pertinent because in the approach of the two religions to other religions they represent the same attitude. Their views of religious knowledge and of the nature of the religious life are similar enough to give them the same method of approach to the problem. In almost anything that one of them says concerning this matter today the other would be in general agreement.

Very early in the development of Hinduism a basic presupposition arose that the Divine manifests itself to individual men or groups of men in diverse ways. It is, as we have seen, the nature of the Divine to do so because the Divine is Itself diverse. God is both unity and diversity, the One and the Many. For the Hindu religious mind it then follows that in the world of diversity in which man is placed, the Divine will be known in Its diverse expressions of Itself. Always insisting upon the basic and fundamental character of unity in its theological-philosophical expressions, Hinduism, nevertheless, gave ready acceptance to diverse apprehensions of that unity. The Rig Veda speaks of the One which is known by many names; the Upanishads continually reiterate this theme, and subsequent Hinduism has accepted it as a dogma of religious thought and practice.

Further, it must be understood that religion reflects man as well as God. Each man is different in that he is at a different stage of religious life and insight. For one man this religious knowledge will be at a level which is far below that of another. Between the high and the low there is room for as many apprehensions of the Divine as there are men to apprehend. Each of these is of value for the individual or group whose religious needs are at that level; each has its place in the totality of the relationship of God and man.

The foregoing does not necessarily mean that each different level or approach is equal in its results. On this point we would find disagreement within and between the two religions. However, this view does represent the confirmed Eastern religious conviction that there is value and worth in any religious belief which gives an individual a consciousness of the true nature of existence, however feeble and mistaken that consciousness may be. Therefore, a tolerance is necessary towards all religious knowledge, and ideally, this tolerance should be of a positive rather than a negative character; that is, it should not be mere acceptance of diversity but it should seek to strengthen the various insights for the common religious good while at the same time lifting that which is considered lower to that which is higher. All who will accept the fundamental presuppositions which we have discussed are to be considered a part of a religious fellowship which is representative of their basic unity of belief and their common religious enterprise.

Contemporary expositions of this theme are being made which are extremely inviting to the modern man in the West. Eastern philosophers and religious thinkers are engaged in a counter-attack against Western religious exclusiveness, and in the process of this attack they are using weapons which are extremely effective among a generation which likes to consider itself tolerant and open-minded. The humanistic flavor of the modern spirit is intrigued by the argument that the insights of all cultures must be weighed by reason and understanding, and it is repelled by appeals to standards which it considers supra-human. This spirit is accustomed to approach and evaluate all things by the light of human reason and it readily looks upon appeals to something beyond reason as being recourses to superstition and ignorance.

A primary factor in the argument from the East, and one which is of great appeal today, is the contention that religion is a matter of personal realization. Certainly it has been characteristic of man in the Western world in the past few centuries to view life as a state in which each individual is challenged to realize his own potentialities to the fullest. America often has been characterized in this way, and Western Europe has been highly influenced by such thought in a growing degree since the Renaissance, Reformation, and the French Revolution. Despite the rapid development of collective thought in many areas of Western life, it would still appear to be correct to say that individual realization and attainment is a central factor in Western thought. If this is true, it is then a simple matter to understand the strength and appeal of the Eastern argument concerning religion among many people of the West.

Personal realization implies the function of individuality, and the inevitable unique diversity which flows from the activities of separate and distinct creative personalities. The modern mind is sufficiently aware of the part played by individual research in the field of the sciences to be greatly intrigued by the suggestion that all men should share in the varied attainments of accomplished individuals in the sphere of religion. This mind and its temper are also not prepared to take the dictates of the past, nor of a certain group. It is seeking Truth and is willing to take Truth wherever it finds it.

Certain things should be made clear, however. The Eastern position is based upon the presupposition that religious knowledge is not the result of one decisive supreme act of the Divine, but it does not exclude divine acts—rather, it affirms them. If it accepts the possibility of the existence of a divine

Being which reveals Itself, the modern secular mind is readily receptive to the Eastern argument. However, the modern Christian is not necessarily fully committed to the contemporary secular mind. The Christian is committed to the belief that the Divine was present and acting in the historic event of Jesus Christ. One would scarcely hazard the statement that the secular humanistic temper in the West today will seriously alter the Christian conviction in this regard. Many nominal Christians, and the more active Christian liberals, may adopt something of the spirit of the Eastern position, but the orthodox core of the Faith will doubtless remain secure in its convictions regarding the divine act in Christ.

It must be noted that the Eastern emphasis upon religion as a matter of personal realization is closely allied with the presupposition that religion is a matter of personal striving. It is on this point as much as any that the Eastern and Western religions differ. The previous chapters pointed to this clear distinction in the religious thought of the two areas, and the fact that both have a place for something of the position of the other does not alter the decisive difference in this feature of religion. Hinduism and a large portion of Buddhism do not discount the self-revealing activity of divinity, and Islam and Christianity do not rule out the necessary religious dedication and activity of individual men. But, the basic emphasis of the two groups of religions is radically different. For the Eastern religions salvation or release is fundamentally an attainment; for the Western, salvation or fulfilment is the result of the gracious act of the Divine. Neither orthodox Christianity nor orthodox Islam can give up their basic beliefs in this regard without destroying the foundations upon which they rest.

The foregoing conflict may be stated in another manner also. For the religions we are discussing, religion is a search for Truth. The difference comes in the manner of the search and, more importantly, in the premises from which the search is begun. The Western religions conceive the search to be a quest for greater understanding and enlightenment of the religious knowledge which is given in the revelations which they have received; the Eastern hold the search to be in the realm of the Unknown, a sphere which is both closed and open to man depending upon his own attainments. In the former it is the search or attempt to come to a further understanding of the Truth that has been given; in the latter it is the quest to be at one with the Truth which is available to all due to the structure of existence, and not to a particular act of divine self-revelation.

The Eastern religions are constantly reiterating their belief that Truth is greater than man's reach and that no particular body of religious belief can be identified with Truth. It is from this that they proceed to insist that it follows that all attainments of man in the sphere of religious insight must be viewed as only approximations rather than the Truth itself. Both Western and Eastern religions have recognized this problem, and all have had in some degree their negative theologies which maintained that God is beyond all human perceptions and mortal statements of His nature. No human term or symbol can be identified with the Divine, since the Divine is greater than any human finite category which can be conceived. Again, the validity of this argument does not alter the Western religious contention which is at the bottom of the conflict between Eastern and Western religions. Despite the fact that the revelations of both Christianity and Islam are in human terms and that these are recognized by most theologians as not being identical with God, they are held to be the results of God's direct activity and intention to the extent that they surpass anything that man himself might conceive. Neither of the Western religions maintains that Truth is within man's grasp, but both insist that Truth is given, and since it is given by God, it is receivable.

We have been attempting to suggest the trend of the answers which Christianity and Islam give to Hinduism and Buddhism at the same time we have presented the Eastern contentions because the arguments and counter-arguments reveal a difference in spirit which lies at the base of the conflict.

To a large extent the views are the same. That which man attains is not to be equated with ultimate Truth. All valid human religious experiences are related to human realization, and human religious attainment is dependent upon human receptivity which ultimately is a result of a divine gift. But these similarities and agreements must not be allowed to obscure the fact that Christianity and Islam are convinced that God has acted in their separate cases as He has not done in that of the other religions. Eastern scholars who make their arguments on the assumption that the above mentioned factors are a ground for agreement, without realizing that ultimately these arguments are of a secondary nature from the viewpoint of their opponents, only deceive themselves with false hopes.

The Hindu approach is one which seeks at the same time to maintain the diversity of religion while holding out for the unity of religion. Hinduism has followed this technique within India and from its own viewpoint has been successful in it. If unity is conceived in a very loose fashion, even the Westerner might agree. However, there are few Christians or Muslims who really know Hinduism who would readily grant that the so-called unity of Hinduism is much more than theory. Certainly at the level of the Hinduism of the masses the world *tolerance* is much more appropriate than unity. Because of their acceptance of a minimal number of the basic Hindu religious presuppositions, including the idea of diversity, widely different religious groups are considered to be a part of the whole of Hinduism. But they are tolerated in a negative fashion; they are not encouraged in active participation within the larger unity and given a deep sense of that unity. Generalizations at this point are extremely hazardous, for the exceptions to this are growing at the present time as Hinduism is actively seeking to develop the unity of which it so often speaks. However, intelligent Hindu leaders are aware that sectarian as well as caste divisions work for disunity, and they are coming to see that diversity is not an unmixed blessing and virtue unless the extent of such diversity is highly limited.

It must be pointed out that the writings and the theories presented in the sphere of the meeting and relationship between religions are in all cases the product of the professionally religious and educated mind. Few Christians have read the books which discuss the Christian approach to the problem, and it is likely that fewer members of the other religions have read their own productions concerning the same issue. Therefore, it often appears to the student from another religion that the author he is reading is presenting an ideal view of his religion and its position in the matter, rather than stating the situation as it really is. Here, again, we are confronted by the problem of the different levels of religion and to what extent they can be taken to represent one another. Does the philosophical-theological mind of Christianity or Islam represent the actual state of the thinking of the peoples of the two religions? Do the highly educated, liberal minded, partially Westernized writers of Hinduism and Buddhism represent the great mass of peoples who are members of the two religions? The caution needs to be made to all groups that they do not accuse the others of speaking ideally while ignoring the great likelihood that they are doing the same. Neither a Hocking, a Kraemer, nor an Amir Ali can be said to be more representative of their respective religions, than can a Radhakrishnan or a Suzuki.

The most forceful and direct statement of the Eastern theory of the relationship between religions in late years has come from Hinduism. On the philosophical-theological level this has been most forcefully stated by Professor Radhakrishnan, one-time professor at Oxford University and now Vice-President of India. Equally at home with the thought of the West and that of the East, he has sought to make the Hindu position clear to the West by an appeal to the tradition of philosophical and scientific inquiry. He has attained a position of great eminence among world philosophers and is considered by scholarly Hindus to be the leading spokesman for the Eastern position. As is the case with most intellectuals, however, the picture he presents of Hinduism and of the Hindu position is one which can hardly be said to reflect contemporary Hinduism at its mass levels. This criticism is made with full cognizance of the warning made in the preceding paragraph that such is very likely true in the cases of the spokesmen for all the religions. However, few Western readers are likely to be aware of the occasional criticisms Professor Radhakrishnan makes of Hinduism, while they are intrigued by the picture he presents of ideal Hinduism as he conceives it. The few Western intellectuals who have been won over by his arguments are not those who are aware of the total and complete nature of Hinduism. They have adopted a philosophical or humanistic position; they have not come to grips with the conflict which is present between great rival religious systems. They neither represent Christianity in its totality as a religion, nor do they have a knowledge of Hinduism as a religion.

On a level which may more properly be called religious than philosophical Hinduism has presented its theory concerning the relationship between religions through a missionary movement which arose in the last decades of the nineteenth century—the Ramakrishna Mission. Receiving its original insights from a Bengali holy man, Ramakrishna, and obtaining its dynamic force from an early leader, Swami Vivekananda, in the last sixty years it has established mission centers in many parts of the Western and Eastern world. While primarily serving as a means for the dissemination of Hindu thought, the message of the Mission is that all religions are true and, therefore, there is no need for any conflict between them. It was the hope of Ramakrishna and Vivekananda that each religion might be revitalized so that it would make the greatest possible contribution to the religious needs and hopes of mankind. Every individual has the possibility of true religious realization by applying himself fully to the religion which is his heritage.

Long reflection upon the theories of the relationship between the leading religions of the world demonstrates that each of these theories is but a further statement of the fundamental convictions out of which the conflict between religions arises. The Eastern theory is a claim that Hinduism and Buddhism are essentially correct in their understanding of religious knowledge; it is made known to man primarily through his own efforts. He may follow the ways of the great saints of the past; he may claim that the teachings of the Vedas or Bhagavad Gita are superior to those of the Tripitika or the Lotus; he may be convinced that the method or way of attainment ultimately is to be found only by following the Jñāna of Shankara, the Bhakti of Rāmānuja, or the Middle Path of the Buddha; he may hold that he is extremely dependent upon the grace of an Avatara or a Bodhisattva—but personal application and attainment of Truth continues to lie at the center of the Eastern religious view. Any real adjustment between religions, any acceptance of the contention that all religions are equal, is to be based upon the fact that they are equal to Hinduism, or equal to Buddhism. The Eastern religions are the criteria by which man is to proceed religiously in the future.

Each theory of adjustment between the conflicting religious systems of the world that is put forward in the West is a reaffirmation of the Western religious belief that ultimately religious knowledge is dependent upon God's self-revealing activity in a series of revelations culminating in a supreme revelation. The religious individual may learn of God in the series of revelations which are the primary property of the Hebrew-Jewish people; he may find religious value in the lives of religious saints and thinkers; he may strengthen his religious insight and way of life by the speculations of philosophers and theologians; he may place greater emphasis upon certain articles of religious belief than do his fellows—but ultimately he must find his supreme source of religious knowledge in one of the two unique self-revelations of God claimed by the two conflicting religions of the West.

It has been considered wise to discuss the theories of adjustment or relationship between religions in terms of East and West, rather than in terms which would specifically apply to each religion. However, such a discussion would not be adequate if mention were not made of the conflicts within the religions themselves over this problem. We are sufficiently aware by now of the differences of thought which exist within the religions and between the religions. The foregoing discussion must not be taken to mean, for example, that Hinduism and Buddhism hold that there is no difference in value between their two religious systems. The Buddhist, whether he be Theravadin or Mahayana, is not ready to allow equal validity to the non-Buddhist Hindu religious system. For example, the Mahayana Buddhist in some instances will feel more at home religiously with the Christian than he will with the Hindu. Again, except in certain realms of philosophy he may have a greater empathy with the Hindu than he does with the Southern Buddhist who is at all orthodox. But he is convinced that the teachings of the Buddha and the insights of historical Buddhism are superior to those of any other religion. The mixture of religious beliefs and practices is so great among the religions that it is difficult in even the most detailed scholarly discussions to differentiate them precisely in a degree that will represent their characteristics adequately.

Nevertheless, at the present time the world is faced with two basic approaches to the problem of the meeting of the world's religions on the part of the religions themselves. There is no reason, and little likelihood, that a choice will be made in the foreseeable future between these two major theories. The religions may well continue to exist side by side with one group of them seeking that one specific religion become the religion of all mankind, and the other group working for the acceptance by all of the validity of all. This is a period for the development of mutual understanding on the part of the religions. The development of modern means of communication; the exchanges of thought; the world-wide economic activity; the supra-regional political alliances; the meeting of the nations in a common political forum; the growing knowledge of the religions and cultures of other peoples—all of these are creating an irresistible force for the development of understanding between religions. Even if the religions desire otherwise, they cannot stem the tide of oneness and unity which is now engulfing the world.

The question which continues to plague mankind, however, is the means whereby this human unity is to be achieved, and the nature of that unity when it comes. If religion is to play the role that many expect of it, and if it is to be a decisive factor in the shaping of the unity which appears to so many to be both desirable and inevitable, it cannot allow the gulf between its various manifestations to continue. The religious separateness of the world may continue for long in the future, but it will do so at great loss to mankind and to religion.

Of course, there are those who are not convinced that unity is the ultimate future of mankind, especially in the immediate centuries that lie ahead. Deeply aware of the powerful forces of regional political groups and political-economic ideologies, they foresee continued conflict between the areas and peoples of the world. This struggle, they believe, will be resolved only by the total victory of one of the powers, or more likely by a chaos in which none will be the victor and mankind will either disappear or return to primitivism.

Confronted by these alternatives, recognizing that they are both distinct possibilities in the future of mankind, and convinced that one or the other is not only possible but probable, thinking men and women of all the world's religions turn to religion expecting it to lead mankind beyond conflict into an era which is only discernible to man in the Religious Knowledge which confronts him in the religions of the world.

VI. *BEYOND CONFLICT*

Discussions concerning the possible contributions of the religions of the world to the amelioration of the problems of mankind are futile and of no significant importance unless the adherents of religion are prepared to face the consequences which may arise from such discussions. It has been our thesis that the world religions are confronted today by two alternatives—continued conflict between themselves in which they all shall suffer, or concrete attempts to come to an understanding and appreciation of each other from which all shall benefit. Those who are convinced that the nature of their religion offers no choice but continued conflict must be prepared for the possibility that not only their own religious faith, but many other values, will disappear as a result of their refusal to join forces with other religiously minded men. Continued conflict between the religions will leave a divided religious world weak before the onslaughts of non-religious forces.

Likewise, those who are convinced that the nature of their religious beliefs and the welfare of mankind demand a deliberate cultivation of understanding and co-operation between religions must see clearly the implications of such action. To what extent will the legitimate demands of their own religious faith allow them to recognize the Religious Knowledge claimed by other religions with whom they seek to work? Are they prepared to face squarely the fact that despite many similarities in the fundamental presuppositions of the major religions there are conflicts which are formidable and far-reaching? And, most important of all, are they fully aware that by embarking on such a course they face the probability that over the years they will be forced to give up certain distinctive claims for their religion which they now hold?

There are those who are committed to both positions, who will deny these suggested consequences of their stand. The former may very well hold that since the religion to which they belong is the result of the activity of the Divine, the Divine will insure the victory of that religion and the defeat of the other religions and the non-religious forces of the world. Even if defeat should come to their religion as a result of the continued conflict between religions, they are firmly convinced that the Divine demands strict loyalty on their part to the Religious Knowledge which He has revealed. Possible defeat must be considered to be either a part of the divine plan or a result of man's failure to measure up to the divine demand. In any case, the Truth would remain, and the Divine would not be defeated in any real or final sense.

The plea for co-operation has often been made by those who are so deeply aware of the similarities between the major religions of the world that they refuse to recognize the fundamental differences which do exist. They are convinced that the similarities are fundamental and the differences peripheral. In this they often reveal themselves to be possessors of an inadequate knowledge of both their own and the other religions. They are not only unscholarly, but naïve in their well-meaning enthusiasm to bring all men together. They would meet the suggested implications of their position by maintaining that since they are seekers after Truth, nothing of real value would have to be given up as a result of the course which they advocate.

There was a time in human history when it was possible for the various religions of the world to escape the necessity of making a decision concerning their actions toward other religions. At the most, they could either ignore each other or depend upon political, military, or cultural forces to settle the problem for them. Today such is not the case. The four major religions which we have been discussing cannot ignore each other without abandoning any claims they have to be of relevance to modern man and his world. The contemporary conception of political and military power is not one which will necessarily further the expansion of religion. And the slow but steady movement of cultural interaction is of such a nature that religion as it is now conceived may very well disappear if it does not seek to influence that interaction in a decisive manner.

One of the greatest difficulties in the sphere of world problems of religion arises from the unconcern of the large majority of religious people with such problems. Their religion appears to them to be satisfying their present religious needs, with the result that they are not moved to look beyond themselves and their immediate community. Despite the tremendous giving toward missions by members of Christian groups, the average Christian in the West cannot be said to be greatly concerned with the missionary program, nor to have evidenced any real concern to be fully acquainted with the nature of the religious beliefs of other peoples. The number of Muslims who have interested themselves in the present world problem of religion is almost negligible. Among the religious peoples of the East such concern is to be found only among the limited few who have had their sights raised beyond their own regional areas.

Nevertheless, the world situation is rapidly bringing about a condition in which this religious provincialism and isolation cannot continue. Among the leadership of the various religions a recognition is growing that new and bold measures must be taken if religion is to achieve its goals in the world that is emerging. For the Christian who is concerned, it is becoming clear that the missionary program of the past, as courageous and dedicated as it was, is not sufficient to meet the problems of today. The few Muslim thinkers who have awakened to the situation are coming to realize that Islam cannot meet its own problems, let alone the challenge of the other religions, without revitalizing its own people and its religious message. The new vitality which is appearing in

Hinduism is bringing certain progressive elements of Hinduism into direct conflict with a conservative orthodoxy and religious lethargy, and the forward movement of the Hindu religion as an influential force beyond its traditional borders depends upon the outcome of the struggle. As with Hinduism, the variety and the disjointed nature of Buddhism makes it difficult to appraise the present attitude of Buddhist leadership, but the past decades have brought concrete attempts on the part of some Buddhist leaders and groups to meet the challenge of the conflict of the world religions.

Each of the world religions approaches the problem equipped with strengths and weaknesses. The decision as to whether a particular aspect of a religion is a strength or detriment in the present situation is fraught with difficulty. What may appear to be a strength to one investigator may very well be considered a weakness to another. For example, the insistence upon ultimate superiority and the refusal to be tolerant of other religious belief on the part of the Western religions gives them a strength which serves as a defense against religious thought and practice from outside themselves. On the other hand, the tolerance and willingness to acknowledge the presence of high values in other religions which is characteristic of some groups within Hinduism and Buddhism can also be held to be a strength in the present struggles between the religions. Two opposite and contradictory features of the world religious scene today are valuable weapons in the struggle between the religions. However, both of these aspects may rightly be seen to be weaknesses for the various religions as they approach the problem of their relationships to each other. Rigidity and final intolerance of all religious faiths but one's own lead to a rejection of attempts at mutual understanding and trust between the religions in which the religion which remains aloof from such attempts suffers more than the religion which seeks such understanding. Contrarily, tolerance and eclectic recognition of religious values from any source have brought about throughout world religious history a weakening of the religion which has not had a clear conception of its own distinctive nature.

Values, strengths, weaknesses, and liabilities are not the paramount factors which must be brought into view in approaching the world religious problem of today. Each religion will be forced by events and its own convictions to appraise its own theories, doctrines, concepts, and practices. It will be confronted by the necessity of determining what it shall retain and what it shall reject. Each religion must determine for itself what its inner essence is—that which is distinctive to it, and which it cannot reject without losing its reason for being. Each religion is responsible for concluding the degree to which its essential nature demands exclusiveness, as well as to what extent that same nature demands purposeful attempts at understanding and empathy for the religious insights of other religions.

At the present stage of religion in the world the phrase "Co-operation without Compromise" would seem to be most appropriate from the perspective of the needs of the day, and the attitudes of the various religions. This conception is one which has been of value in the West in those areas where separate religious groups have sought to work together. It has arisen from a recognition that without co-operation certain areas of common concern will be neglected to the detriment of religion and those it seeks to serve. It is an outcome of the realization that while complete unity cannot be achieved, yet total separation is folly and self-defeating. More than one competent investigation of Western society and its problems has pointed to the heightening of those problems by a divided religious witness which has not possessed the strength to resist the onslaught of non-religious forces within the society.

The contribution which the religions of the world can make to contemporary man and his society can only be made when the religions rise above their present state of conflict with each other. If, and when, they are willing to give up their momentary claims in order that they may ultimately bring about their fundamental aims, then, and only then, will the world religions be prepared to make the necessary contribution to the present human situation which is demanded both by the needs of man and the very nature of the religions themselves.

Religious programs which are concerned with the establishment of a particular religion among all men without regard to the present religious convictions or conditions of mankind, are founded upon a false premise because they do not take into account the present situation wherein such cannot be accomplished without the use of compulsion. Religious compulsion resulting in religious uniformity is not only impossible in the present world scene, but it is counter to the religious spirit of today as well. This does not mean that peaceful missionary programs undertaken with due regard for the religious sensitivities and traditions of a people are to be abandoned. It does not mean that men of one religious faith are to cease in their efforts to share their beliefs with those who are outside their religion. What it does mean is that there must be a determined attempt on the part of each of the world religions to come to an understanding of the religious heritage and aspirations of the other religions.

If the religions of the world were to recognize their common interest in the development of a united religious witness to humanity and contemporary society, the impact of such a witness upon the age in which we live could well be the most decisive factor in the settlement of the problems of the present, and the shaping of the immediate future. If the religions do not do so, humanity is confronted by the necessity of continuing to rely upon religions which by their actions are failing to achieve the greatness of which they are capable. From the perspective of the Western religions, the divine mission with which they have been entrusted would appear to demand that they embark upon a program which will bring to more men and women the Truth which is their most precious possession. So too, the Eastern religions cannot be true to themselves unless they are prepared to share their insights into the nature of Truth with all mankind. What is needed at the moment is the development of a spirit of understanding and co-operative purpose which will serve as an atmosphere conducive to the growth of concrete programs whereby the religions of both the East and the West can confront man in his present predicament with the combined challenge of religion in its highest and most dynamic form.

Toward a United Witness

Our discussions of the conflict between the basic presuppositions of the leading religions have indicated that each of them approaches similar fundamental theoretical problems from a perspective which is singularly its own. The differences between the religions, and the sources for much of their conflict, arise out of the cluster of presuppositions and the spiritual perceptivity which is uniquely their own. This uniqueness exists despite the presence in a religion of much that has come from outside itself. Such outside influences and beliefs do not become integral to a religion until they have undergone the process of becoming a unity with the specific essence of the religion.

Mysticism is the most obvious example of a factor which is present in each of the leading religions, which evidences a history of cross influence between the religions, and which, nevertheless, has in each instance succeeded in adapting itself to each of the religions in such a manner that it may be said to be an integral part of the totality of the religion. Despite the fact that there are Christians and Muslims who will deny that mysticism as usually defined has a place in either of their religions, an objective study of Christianity and Islam will establish that some of the greatest figures in their history were mystics. The fact that they may have been classed as heretics by others of their religion does not alter the significance and value of mystical experience in their total religious life. The point of importance is that because the mystical experience is of value in the religious life, each of the religions has brought its own expression of mysticism into line with its basic presuppositions. As a result, each of the religions has been enriched by the presence of mystics who were completely devoted to the fundamental beliefs of their own religion.

However, all too many enthusiasts for the establishment of a harmony, and possible unity, between the religions have assumed that there is no fundamental difference between the expressions of mysticism in the separate religions. They have used mysticism as an example of the existence in the various religions of an identical phenomenon upon which can be built a universal religion to which all religions can give their support. They have failed to understand that, as with all other aspects of religion, the mysticism in the separate religions cannot be understood adequately on the basis of universal mysticism but only in its relationship to the fundamental presuppositions of the religion of which it is a part. The theories of Religious Knowledge, the Divine, Man, Human Fulfilment —each of these play their part in making the particular mysticism what it is. Despite the fact that mystics often are able to discern values in other religions, values which usually are ignored by non-mystics, each mystic remains a part of his own religious heritage and its presuppositions. To disassociate himself from them would be to destroy the grounds upon which his mystical experience rests. Saint John of the Cross and Meister Eckhart were *Christians* first, and then mystics. Al Hallaj and Rabia were led to their mysticism because of the profound sense of the Divine which was given them by the revelation of the Divine in the *Koran*. Shankaracharya and Ramakrishna were mystics because they were *Hindus* and because they were committed to the fundamental presuppositions which are the foundation of the Hindu apprehension of Truth. The mystics of Buddhism from the earliest times down to modern Zen have in each case been *Buddhist* mystics whose thought, insights, and aspirations cannot be disassociated from the fundamental presuppositions of their religion.

Any attempts which may be made to develop an understanding between the religions whereby they will be enabled to embark upon programs of united religious witness must proceed from a clear understanding of this individual nature of each religion and its components. The refusal of well-meaning enthusiasts to recognize differences between the religions as important actualities, rather than inconsequential non-entities, only serves to defeat their aims. When it is recognized that each religion is an entity unto itself, as well as a phenomenon which is related to all other religious phenomena, then the development of understanding and co-operation between the respective religions can progress on a firm foundation. Individual religious presuppositions and insights will be respected and understood in the light of their true significance as constituent parts of a total system of religious apprehension and yearning.

A. THE PRIMARY AFFIRMATIONS

The theories of Religious Knowledge, the Divine, Man, and Human Fulfilment which are fundamental to the great religions, can serve as a solid foundation for the development of understanding between the religions. If the differences between the presuppositions of the religions are clearly discerned and kept in mind, it will be possible for religious thinkers to probe deeply into the thought of the separate religions without losing the distinctive spirit and contribution of each of the religions. And, even more important, the total impact of the combined witness of the separate religions to their firm beliefs in regard to the Divine and man's relationship to It, can serve all of the religions in their conflict with the currents of modern thought and life which tend to depreciate or deny the primary claims of religion concerning the Divine.

The challenge of modern secularism to the various religions is directly related to the emphasis which the secular spirit places upon the self-sufficiency of man in his individuality, or in community. This emphasis, which to a large degree is the outgrowth of the humanism and liberalism of the past centuries, has been of particular importance in the development of modern Western civilization. Through the penetration of Western thought and ways of living into the East it has now become a definite factor in the new and developing ethos of the non-Western areas. The benefits to man and society which have arisen as a result of this humanistic emphasis are so marked that Christianity in particular has often found itself a part of the movement. In fact, the impetus towards much of modern secularism has arisen from the Christian emphasis upon the individuality and dignity of man.

Nevertheless, as a result of this stress upon man's self-sufficiency, the central contention of the major religions of the world—that man is a related and derivative being who can never be considered correctly apart from his relationship with his fellows, and from his ultimate connection with something beyond the world—has suffered. The belief in the self-sufficiency of man has caused man to look to himself for his own fulfilment, and it has led him to believe that his fulfilment is limited to his existence on the earth. As a result, man's fellow beings are to be used primarily as means for his own fulfilment, and the idea of a Divine, or even a structure of existence such as is suggested by Theravadin Buddhism, is denied.

The world religions stand in opposition to any view which holds that man is sufficient unto himself, either in his living of his earthly life or in the achievement of his ultimate destiny. The Western religions are founded upon the conviction that man is of a derivative character, and that he can only be understood in the light of his dependence upon the Divine. The Eastern religions, despite their emphasis upon the part that man must play in attaining salvation, are united in their conviction that there are forces outside himself which man must take into account in his earthly life and in his desire to achieve fulfilment. Whether these forces are considered to be the Divine Itself, or whether they are simply eternal laws which govern existence, they are of a character which declares that man is not totally and completely dependent upon himself. Even the most highly developed forms of Theravadin Buddhism refuse to limit man's concern to himself alone, nor do they see man's fulfilment as being limited to this world.

Together the religions of the world confront the secular spirit of the modern day with the challenge that man look beyond himself and his present environment for the ultimate meaning and fulfilment which he seeks. They insist that man is meant for something more than merely a brief existence on this earth, or simply a continuous round of earthly existences. In the first instance, they urge man to consider his present state as but the beginning of a total experience which will lift him far beyond that which he now knows. In the second, they call upon man to escape from the limited existence which he now experiences to the condition of non-being which far surpasses the circumscribed life of man in the world.

The confusion of the conflicting claims of separated religions causes modern man to ignore their challenge and to seek meaning and fulfilment in those aspects of existence which are close at hand and more easily understood. While it is true that man is prone to attach himself to the material factors of existence which he can measure, manipulate, and therefore partially understand, yet he seldom finds full satisfaction in them. The history of humanity cannot be limited to a recital of the advancement of man's knowledge concerning the material world in which he lives; nor can it be measured by the development of civilizations which have conquered some of man's problems in the ever-present struggle for physical existence and well-being. On the contrary, human history is fundamentally the record of man's persistent search for meaning in life, and for the creation of a consistent system of thought which makes the struggle of existence a purposeful and worthwhile endeavor. Despite his proclivity to immerse himself in the close-at-hand material problems of his existence, and the fact that he sometimes tends to lose an active consciousness of anything beyond this sphere, man finds himself irresistibly drawn to the challenge of the Divine which confronts him in the witness of the world's religions.

There is no level of human concern with the meaning of

life which is not met by the combined Religious Knowledge of the world's religions. At every stage of human spiritual and intellectual development the religions possess insights which both inspire and challenge men with visions of something beyond the limited boundaries which encompass them in their physical existence. So-called low levels of religion exist because there are men at levels of intellectual and spiritual attainment whose conscious needs are met only by them. The philosopher or theologian must also find meaning for life, and understanding of that which lies at the center of physical existence, and for him there is a challenge coming from the combined witness of the religions of the world. No philosopher of note in any area of the world can ignore the thought of the religions in their theoretical expressions, even if he proposes systems of thought which contradict them. Even in his opposition he is forced by the historic and human environment which surrounds him to depend upon theological presuppositions which have played a positive or negative role in the development of all systems of philosophy.

But, more important, the Religious Knowledge which is the combined possession of the great religions—diversified, and sometimes contradictory, as it is—is a witness to modern confused man that he can, if he will, rise above his present limitations. It is the message of the world religions that there is available to man a knowledge which will enable him to conquer his personal and social problems. There is a Truth which surpasses the apparent truth which man can find in his physical world by his rational ability. This Truth is neither inherently irrational nor supra-rational; but it is of a nature which cannot be adequately fathomed simply by total reliance upon the usual mental processes and abilities, for it calls upon the religious sensitivities as well as the rational powers of man.

At the moment it is not the primary concern of man as to by what means this knowledge has come to the religions which present it. The over-riding anxiety is whether it does contain the Truth—a Truth which is adequate to meet the present needs of man and his society—or whether it is simply another human pretension to knowledge which will be found insufficient when it is brought face to face with the realities of existence which man cannot escape in his present predicament. It is not the primary task of the religions to demonstrate the validity of their separate presuppositions as to how they obtained the knowledge which they possess; rather, it is their function to challenge mankind with the Truth present in the knowledge. When this is done, and only then, man individually and in community can embark upon the ever-enriching path of life to which the religions point.

The more enlightened conceptions of religion and spiritual values of today, and the needs of humanity, are such that the individual religions must cease in their contentions regarding the relative worth of the methods by which they have obtained their Religious Knowledge and the Truth which is contained within it. This does not mean that it should not remain of concern to the adherents of separate religions as to whether the particular knowledge which is their heritage is superior or inferior to that of other religions. It does mean, however, that such a concern must be removed from the front line of the message of the religions, and reserved for the non-contentious atmosphere of quiet reflection and meditation which is the heart of the individual religious experience and its enrichment. The struggle with Truth at this level must be reserved for the quiet and harmonious atmosphere which Truth demands; it cannot be brought into the area of open struggle for men's minds and affections without the loss of the Truth Itself.

Each of the religions is convinced that the Religious Knowledge which is fundamental to it is of incalculable value to man in the present situation which confronts him. The Western religions hold that the Truth contained in their separate messages is not concerned only with the future non-worldly state of man. On the contrary, the Christian gospel and the Islamic message concerning Allah, are filled with injunctions as to how man should approach the problems of his personal earthly life and community relationships. Hinduism and Buddhism may ultimately place less stress upon life in the physical world (though this would be denied by many of both religions), yet the whole fabric of their messages to man is woven around the conception that how man lives, and the goals he seeks, in his present life are determinative factors in the attainment of his ultimate fulfilment beyond this life.

As a result of their conviction that they are the carriers of knowledge which is of value to man, it is incumbent upon the world religions that they use every legitimate resource in bringing that knowledge to man in the present age. The solution of the difficulties of individual man and of society, and the survival of the knowledge of the values contained in Religious Knowledge hang in the balance. If the separate religions cannot themselves come to see the related nature and extreme value of their knowledge of the Divine, Man, and Human Fulfilment, they cannot expect the modern man to be greatly concerned with it. If they are devoting so much of their energies to the conflict which arises out of the legitimate differences between their respective messages, they can have little hope of challenging humanity with the Truth and value which also are present.

The importance of the convictions concerning Religious Knowledge which are held by the leading religions lies in the direct challenge they present to much of the current thought and practice of man and his society. The combined impact of the theories of Religious Knowledge, and the central significance of any conception of Religious Knowledge for humanity today, are in the fact that modern man is confronted by the sincere belief of his religious contemporaries that the divisions and conflicts between separate groups of humanity are founded upon misconceptions concerning man and the nature of society. It is the nature of Religious Knowledge that it is founded upon the conviction that there is more for man to know than simply that which is necessary for the maintenance of his physical body. In each case, while not necessarily depreciating the material life of man, the theories of Religious

Knowledge held by the separate religions point firmly to the conviction that the fundamental worth of human existence lies not in human concern for the physical necessities of life, but in the development of the spiritual potentialities of man.

It is in the separate theories of Religious Knowledge that the decisive *raison d'etre* of the religions, and the ultimate reason for hope from religion for modern man and society, are revealed. We have discussed the different theories of the Divine sufficiently to make clear that they cannot all be lumped together into a unity without doing violence to the convictions of each of the religions concerning the Divine. Nor can we ignore the negative or atheistic presuppositions concerning the Divine which is in Theravadin Buddhism. However, even including these differences, it is obvious that the four major religions of the world, despite their internal and external conflicts, are united in confronting man with the Truth that there is an existent Source of being upon which man is dependent, which he must take into consideration in the living of his present life, and to which he must look for his ultimate fulfilment. In either of its major forms Buddhism insists that man must order his life and his society in accordance with the given nature of existence which rises from Dharma, the Law of Karma, and the constituent factors within man. Man is called upon to refuse to dedicate himself to the desires, selfishness, and egoism which arise from his confusion of the transitory real for the Eternal Real. In all of its religious manifestations, Hinduism makes a similar demand at various levels commensurate with the intellectual stature and religious environment of the Indian people. Islam confronts man with the demand that he submit himself to the Real which is the source of all that is, including man himself. In a degree seldom equalled in the other religions, it reminds man of his dependence upon the Divine in all that he does and assures him that by living a life of submission to the Divine, the Compassionate Allah will guide his actions and reward his faith in this world and the next. Christianity calls upon man to put himself in right relationship with the Divine and to live his life in the manner which is demanded by the revelation which the Divine has given of Himself and His will for man.

In each case, then, the religions are united in theory, if not in practice, in calling upon man to recognize that his nature is such that he, his present well-being, and his future fulfilment are directly related to the Religious Knowledge which they possess, and to the Divine or supra-human Real of existence to which they each witness. It is at this point above all that the world religions have a resource for rising above their present inter-religious conflict, and meeting the challenge of the Spirit of the Times.

The conflict between religion and the modern secular spirit is a struggle which arises from the secular rejection of the primacy of the Divine, or non-physical, which is at the heart of the Religious Knowledge possessed by the religions. The great majority of religious interpreters of the dilemma of modern man and his society maintain that it is due to this rejection of the supreme place of the Divine in human life and community that the events and conditions of today are so terrifying to mankind. The situation which confronts man is the result of man's disavowal of his intimate relationship with a supra-human element in existence, and its seeming gargantuan and insoluble nature is the consequence, not of the situation itself, but of the insufficiency of man which comes from his radical disavowal of the Divine. The political movements, the economic systems, the well intentioned but never sufficient programs devised by man—all these fall short because of the estrangement between man and the Divine. The destructive egoistic impulses of individuals; the ruinous self-exaltation of small and large groups; the ravaging and cataclysmic conflicts between groups of men—these are present in human life as a result of man's refusal to pattern his life in conformity with the divine demand revealed in the Religious Knowledge which is present in the world religions.

By their combined witness to mankind, the religions of the world point the way whereby men may face their present situation with courage, and with programs which are suffi-

cient for the overcoming of a total situation which threatens
to destroy men and their aspirations. If the leading world
religions are prepared to work together in bringing about the
objectives they have in common, and if they are willing to
approach their own differences in a spirit of understanding
rather than conflict, the possibility of the relief of the world
from the misery and fear which now engulfs it would appear
to be closer to realization that ever before in human history.

More important, however, is the vision of the degree to
which much of the message of the individual religions would
be established in human minds and affections. True, there
are some who would maintain that this is a hope which ignores the realities of human frailty. Because of their theological convictions, and their resultant beliefs concerning the
nature of man, they will hold that even the best united witness to the religious spiritual nature of man and his relationship to the Divine, will not be sufficient to lift man out of the
degradation to which he has descended as a result of his
alienation from the Divine. It should be sufficient to remind
them that while a united witness by the world's religions is
not a panacea for all the world's ills, yet any theological position worthy of their religion (whatever it may be) demands
that they seek to do all possible to make men aware of their
present state and their potential fulfilment beyond it. Each of
the religions is committed to the endeavor to share its Religious Knowledge with as many men as possible. With the
exception of few periods and groups in its history, Christianity has considered it to be its greatest task to bring the
gospel of Christ to people within and without its own geo-
graphical boundaries. The most stirring periods in Muslim
history have been those in which Islam has sought to bring
the revelation of the Koran to more people, and the most
fruitful years have been those in which Muslim religious
genius has been applied to the development of systematic and
penetrating expositions of it. Of the four religions under discussion, Hinduism is the only one which has not purposefully
embarked upon a foreign missionary program, yet throughout

all of its history it has been engaged in the process of sharing its highest insights with the many and varied peoples of the Indian sub-continent. Today one of the most important facts in the contemporary world religious and cultural scene is the appearance of Hinduism as a religion with a consciousness of a mission outside its traditional borders. The history of Buddhism, in both its forms, is the record of the dissemination of the knowledge of the Enlightenment of the Buddha and the proclamation of the Way of the Middle Path over vast and dissimilar areas of the East.

By their separate efforts over the centuries, the leading religions of the modern world have given mankind a glimpse of what human society and individual personality can be when it is conscious of the religious element within existence as revealed in the higher expressions of Religious Knowledge possessed by these religions. There are few men of any time or place who are not stirred by the lives of the great saints of religion, and by the visions of peaceful and purposeful society which each of the religions has established at least in minia-ture at some time in its history. At the present juncture of world history, humanity appears to possess the material and institutional tools whereby much of the social longings of men can be fulfilled. Yet it is at this same time, and by the use of these same tools, that man is now fearful lest all he cherishes be destroyed.

In the realm of human personality and spiritual enrichment, humanity also possesses much that it has not had in past cen-turies. The present knowledge of psychology, the ever-widen-ing opportunity for education, the means for the mass dis-semination of the cultural arts—these and other factors give man opportunity for personal growth which at best was limited to the few in the past. But here again, man is filled with a sense of frustration and despair to a degree seldom before equalled in human history. All of these opportunities only mock man by giving him hope but denying him fulfil-ment. The liberal and humanitarian spirit of the past centuries which has so largely motivated society in the West now appears to be disappearing amid a rising tide of cynicism. A growing tendency to curtail the individual freedom of the human personality for the announced purpose of gaining material security is causing the withdrawal of the self from its neighbors. Rather than the creation of a world order composed of enlightened human beings, man is deeply conscious of the all too likely disappearance of even the regional and relative political and economic security which is now his.

All of this points to the inability of man to use the products of his genius for the fulfilment of his ultimate aims. There is no need to belabor the point further, for this has been made clear enough in multitudes of writings, as well as in the very events of recent and contemporary history. It is this situation which the religions of the world must face with realism, and with the consciousness that it is in their power to lift man out of the despair which now engulfs him. Each of the religions is convinced that individually it possesses such power, but it suffers from a delusion as tragic as that of man if it does not perceive that alone it can accomplish little, while in a united witness with the other religions on those fundamentals which are essential to all, and which are desperately needed by contemporary man, it can accomplish much.

Beyond conflict, Buddhism, Hinduism, Islam, and Christianity can find a harmony in the fundamental presuppositions which lie at the base of their separate structures. If they recognize that this harmony is not all-embracing, but yet is fundamental and essential, and if they are willing to forget past conflicts in an enthusiasm for new accomplishment and greater service, these religions can lead mankind out of the darkness of today into the light of tomorrow. By their invitation to man to lift his eyes beyond himself they can defeat the political-philosophical-social-technological secularism which now threatens to destroy them and that for which they stand.

B. THE INITIAL PRINCIPLES

The ultimate aims of the world religions, and the present condition of mankind, challenge the individual religions to

new thinking and pioneer action rather than a continuation
of the inter-religious conflict in which they have been engaged. The religions are called to a united witness to those
concepts and values which in their separate ways they seek
to inculcate in individual personal life and in human society.
Where previously the regional and provincial nature of human society may have called for a separate witness by the
religions, today the ultimate purposes of the religions are
hindered by their continued habit of provincial and self concern.

Those groups within the separate religions which are aware
of the challenge, and which are prepared to confront it, are
faced with the necessity of enlarging their influence among
adherents of their own religion, while at the same time they
seek for practical measures whereby they can establish rapport with others of similar convictions in the other religions.
Those who are Christians and Muslims will face the determined and sincere opposition of their fellows who are convinced that their respective religions are of such a nature that
actual religious co-operation with other religions is apostasy
of the worst kind. While those who are Hindu and Buddhist
will find less theological opposition for a program of co-
operation with other religions, they will also be met with the
sincere conviction of many of their fellow religionists that it
is only by witness to the Truths of their separate religions
that they can fulfil their religious duty to mankind. Nevertheless, it has always been the responsibility of pioneers to face
the disapproval and the warnings of those who are not inspired with the vision which moves them.

Specific programs cannot be formulated and then imposed
upon those who would seek to co-operate. Rather, they must
rise out of the collective aspirations of those seeking to make
religion effective in the life of world humanity. The potential
good of such action, the strains and stresses which will be
placed upon the separate religions, and the individual faith
of the participants must be fully recognized by all who desire
to support a united world religious witness. Beyond this, no

one can go at the present moment in maintaining that they will co-operate in this matter, but they will not co-operate in some other endeavor. If the combined witness of the world's religions is to mean anything at all, it must be founded upon the understanding that all parties must enter into the endeavor fully conscious of their differences, but prepared to co-operate to the fullest extent that their religious consciences will allow. It will be only when once the fundamental understanding is achieved that the limits to which individual religions or members of the religions can go will become clear.

However, there are certain basic principles which would appear to be worthy of consideration as sensitive religious men seek to develop the understanding necessary for the victory of the religious ideal among all peoples around the world. These principles are neither new nor startling to those who have studied the history of man's religions, and who are acquainted with the various attempts which have been made in the direction of inter-religious co-operation and understanding. These principles would appear to be absolutely indispensable to any practical development which will escape the naïve unscholarly approach which has marked so many appeals to inter-religious understanding.

First, there is the obvious necessity of purposeful attempts to develop means whereby an *exchange of thought* between the religions can come about. By this is meant an exchange of thought for purposes of investigation and knowledge, not an exchange wherein any of the religions will adopt some aspect of the thought of another of the religions. Despite the progress which has been made in this direction in the past century by the development of academic disciplines which are concerned with the various religions and cultures of mankind, the great majority of the people of the world have little factual knowledge of the religious beliefs and systems of other peoples. What knowledge they do possess is very often so incomplete that they totally misunderstand the religious spirit which motivates other religions. Aware only of what we have termed the "lower levels" of foreign religions, they have failed to acquaint themselves with the high and valuable thought which is usually discernible only after more detailed study. And, as we have indicated previously, there are others who need to be made aware of the total unified and unique nature of each religion so that they do not continue in their mistaken assumption that all religions are ultimately the same —either in their present content or in their ultimate aims.

Of all the basic principles which must underlie the attempt to replace the past and present conflict between the religions with a spirit of understanding and co-operation, the exchange of knowledge concerning the religions is the most fundamental. Ignorance leads to fear, misunderstanding, and conflict; while knowledge leads to appreciation, understanding of the fundamental differences and agreements, and a correct realization of what is necessary for worthwhile and productive co-operation. The development of regional and cultural studies in various universities around the world; the growth of the study of the History of Religions; the expanding production of literature relating to the religions and cultures of the world; the exchange of students between countries—these and other factors are contributing to the exchange of thought which must precede and implement any program of interreligious understanding and co-operation.

The world religions can contribute to the development of this exchange—and, indeed, they have done so to a limited degree—by sponsoring, wherever possible, the study of the other religions by their own adherents. Even if they are to continue their conflict, it is necessary for them to know the nature of their adversary; and if they have come to any realization at all of what we have been attempting to demonstrate, they should be aware of the need to know more of their possible allies. Others have attempted to discuss in detail the establishment of centers of study where adherents of different religions can come together to gain knowledge of the religious faiths which each possesses. This is a specific program which can only be workable and brought into fruition when there is sufficient sentiment within two or more religions to support such a move. It would be the logical outcome of the recognition of the need for the sharing of thought which is essential to any successful co-operative enterprise between two or more persons.

Secondly, a basic principle which must be recognized by all who seek to bring about the cessation of inter-religious conflict and the establishment of co-operation is that there must be some place in any program which may be developed for *common worship and spiritual fellowship.* Religion is not simply a matter of intellectual assent or social conformity. The nature of religion demands that those who are a part of it develop within themselves an ability for worship and spiritual reflection; in fact, one is not a part of a religion until this aspect of the religious life has become an integral portion of his religious activity. There is a place for individual worship and for collective worship. Those who would enter into fellowship with others of different religious faiths must be prepared to join in common worship, or the fellowship will not be of a religious nature.

There immediately will be some, especially in the Western religions, who will be aware of the problems involved for those who are members of the strictly monotheistic religions. Here, again, what is needed is the recognition that spiritual fellowship is necessary to the implementation of the co-operation between religions which is desired, as well as being a rewarding experience for all those who take part in it. The forms such worship and fellowship will take, and the degree to which members of the different faiths will participate, are matters which, as we have suggested, cannot be determined until the grounds for the fellowship are discovered in a common dedication to the task of presenting the united witness of the world's religions. When sincere religious men and women of different faiths are bound together in a common task to which they are highly dedicated, the most natural result of their spiritual dedication to a common task will be the discovery of means of worship and fellowship whereby they are enriched and fortified for their task. If they enter into such a fellowship sufficiently grounded in their knowledge of their own faith and the religious convictions of others, they will be able to work out together the manner of worship in which they can co-operate to the enrichment of all.

A third principle which cannot be ignored in any serious endeavor for a united religious witness to modern man is one which involves the proclamation of a *religious ethical standard*. In our discussion of the leading religions we have not investigated their ethical systems. Nevertheless, their fundamental presuppositions should give us an awareness of the inevitable ethical teachings which have arisen as a result of religious convictions concerning the Divine, Man, and Human Fulfilment. Each religion possesses an ethical system. The individual systems are correlated with the fundamental essence of each religion, and cannot be separated from the unique nature of the religion which supports them. The ethics of the leading religions are not the same, nor can it be said that the emphasis upon ethical behavior is the same in the different religions.

However, despite the differences, each of the religions has an ethical witness to make to the contemporary world which must lie at the very heart of any religious message which will meet today's problems. Christianity's conviction that the Divine has revealed standards of justice which must be met by man; Islam's emphasis upon the brotherhood demanded by the Divine in human relationships; Hinduism's concern that all men recognize their common relationship with the Divine; Buddhism's stress upon tenderness and compassion for all life—these are ideals which are as greatly needed by men today as at any time in history. And it will be noted that these conceptions are not limited to the religions with which we have just placed them in the previous sentence. Rather, in one form or another most of them are to be found in each of the religions.

Each of the religions has a place for the conception of proper and improper actions which are important both in personal living and in community relationships. From the perspective of one of the religions the ethical standards of another may appear to be based upon false premises and to fall far short of the standards and ideals which it possesses. Of course, this is also true in regard to much of the theory and practice of all the religions as they are viewed by each other. Yet it is to be doubted whether anyone who is acquainted with the higher ethical teachings of the individual religions would question the desirability that those ideals be dynamically presented to modern man. The sincerely and religiously ethical man of all the great religions is sorely needed in the world today. Those who are active participants in the separate religions are confronted by the necessity of continued personal striving to reach the heights of ethical thought and conduct which are the legacy of their faiths. Those who are not actively religious are often in their best moments aware that their ideals and standards of conduct do not measure up to what they expect of themselves, nor what they would desire in others.

The ethical demands of religion cannot be separated from the message which religion has for man concerning the Divine and man's relationship to the Divine. No matter what the Divine is considered to be, and even where the Divine in the usual sense is denied, there are ideals of conduct, and standards of thought which inevitably flow from the Religious Knowledge which is at the foundation of each of the religions. The problems of contemporary man and his society possess much of their difficulty because individual men and women have failed to govern their lives by standards other than those which arise from their own immediate needs. Any co-operative witness by the world religions which will furnish man with the necessary resources for the meeting of those problems will of necessity be one which has ethical content.

Finally, once there is agreement between responsible groups of the leading religions as to the need of co-operative witness, they must be guided by the principle of *co-operation in freedom*. Nothing serves to defeat the purposes of religion, and the spiritual needs of men, more than the conceptions of uniformity and compulsion. Past suggestions concerning the development of world religious movements or systems have generally fallen down at this point. In early centuries they were most often based on an idea of compulsion, and even in more modern times there has been a failure to be aware of both the impossibility and the undesirability of uniformity.

There are few, if any, religious persons who are aware of the necessity for a united witness of the values of religion to the world, who would advocate any form of religious compulsion. They are conscious not only that compulsion runs counter to the essence of religion, but they also recognize that compulsion in the sphere of religion, as in most other matters, is defeating of the very aims the compulsion seeks to bring about. It is here that the religions have a most powerful strength in their conflict with the political-secular movements which are in opposition to religion. The religions appeal to the free spirit of man, while their opponents offer man a false security at the expense of a real slavery. The latter appeal to the self-gaining instincts, while the former challenge the higher self-giving qualities of man.

Uniformity must not be thought of except in the broadest possible connotation. The co-operation in freedom which must underlie the united witness of religion is a co-operation which will rise from a unity of purpose and general conviction, and not from a uniformity of thought and practice. No realistic movement to erase the conflict between the religions will insist upon a uniformity of thought and practice among the religions. Such has not been possible even within the individual religions, and it is certainly not conceivable in the wider and more varied context of the religions of the world.

More important, the principle of co-operation in freedom will give the needed atmosphere for the fullest expression of the unique nature of each of the religions within the wide and stimulating fellowship which will be afforded by the separate religions no longer in conflict. In this fellowship of mutual exchange and understanding the element of freedom will enable the separate religions to delve more deeply into the essence of their own nature. They will be spurred on by the stimulus of the knowledge and friendship of others of different faiths, and they will come to know in a greater degree that sense of religious depth and dedication which comes from fellowship with religious men and women.

The leading religions are confronted today by a choice of co-operation in a spirit of freedom and understanding, or of continued conflict in an atmosphere of suspicion and fear. The future of both religion and mankind depends upon the choice they shall make. And most important of all, the establishment in the life and affection of mankind of the values which they have received from the Source of their Religious Knowledge hangs in the balance. Can there be any real question as to the choice they must make?

SUGGESTED READINGS

I. Religion in the West

Amīr Ali, *The Spirit of Islam* (London, 1922).

H. A. R. Gibb, *Modern Trends in Islam* (Chicago, 1947).

M. Iqbāl, *The Reconstruction of Religious Thought in Islam* (Oxford, 1943).

E. J. Jurji (ed.), *The Great Religions of the Modern World* (Princeton, 1946), pp. 284–370.

H. R. Niebuhr, *Christ and Culture* (New York, 1951).

G. F. Thomas (ed.), *The Vitality of the Christian Tradition* (New York, 1944).

A. J. Toynbee, *Civilization on Trial* (New York, 1948), pp. 184–212.

II. Religion in the East

E. J. Jurji (ed.), *The Great Religions of the Modern World* (Princeton, 1946), pp. 44–140.

K. W. Morgan (ed.), *The Religion of the Hindus* (New York, 1953).

J. B. Pratt, *The Pilgrimage of Buddhism* (London, 1928).

S. Radhakrishnan, *Eastern Religions and Western Thought* (Oxford, 1939).

III. The Conflict Between Religions: Religious Knowledge and the Divine

J. Baillie and H. Martin (ed.), *Revelation* (London, 1937).

H. Bhattacharyya, *The Foundations of Living Faiths* (Calcutta, 1938).

E. Brunner, *Revelation and Reason,* translated by O. Wyon (London, 1947).

B. Kumarappa, *Hindu Conceptions of Deity* (London, 1934).

IV. The Conflict Between Religions: Man and Human Fulfilment

John C. Bennett, *Christian Realism* (New York, 1941), pp. 46–73.

Sydney Cave, *Redemption: Hindu and Christian* (London, 1919).

Reinhold Niebuhr, *The Nature and Destiny of Man*, 2 vols. (New York, 1941–43).

Robert L. Slater, *Paradox and Nirvana* (Chicago, 1951).

V. Western and Eastern Theories of Reconciliation

E. C. Dewick, *The Christian Attitude to Other Religions* (Cambridge, 1953).

W. E. Hocking, *Living Religions and a World Faith* (New York, 1940).

H. Kraemer, *The Christian Message in a Non-Christian World* (New York, 1937).

S. Radhakrishnan, *The Hindu View of Life* (London, 1927).

Albert Schweitzer, *Christianity and the Religions of the World* (New York, 1923).

A. J. Toynbee, *Civilization on Trial* (New York, 1948), pp. 213–252.

H. V. White, *A Theology for Christian Missions* (New York, 1937).

INDEX

Adaptation, 174
al-Afghāni, Jamāl al-Din, 27
al Hallaj, 199
Ali, 32 f.
Allah, 38 f., 74, 81 ff., 102 ff.,
    105 f., 129, 130 ff., 132 f.,
    152 ff.
Amir Ali, 187
Anatta doctrine, 142
Anglican, 14, 17
Anglo-Catholic, 14
Arhant, 69
Aryan invasions, 85
Ātman, 108, 136 ff.
Avataras, 87 f., 158, 189

Bhagavad Gita, 51, 157, 189
Bhagavat, 157 f.
Bhakti, 163, 189
Bhakti marga, 155–162, 165
Bodhisattva, 69 f., 115 ff.,
    165 f., 189
Brahman, 85 ff., 107 ff., 135 ff.,
    160
Brotherhood, 35
Buddha; *see* Gautama Buddha
Buddhism, 60–71, 90–94, 111–
    120, 142–146, 162–167,
    180 ff.
  attitude toward world, 63 ff.
  attitudes toward other reli-
    gions, 180 ff.
  Bodhi (Enlightenment), 91
    ff., 167

in conflict, 60–71
contemporary, 195
dependent origination, 143
the Divine, 111–120
heavens, 163
hells, 163
human fulfilment, 162–167
Karma, 144 f.
laymen, 66–70, 163
Mahayana, 46, 67 ff., 93 f.,
    111, 114–119, 163 ff., 190
man, 142–146
reform, 44 f.
religious knowledge, 90–94
renaissance, 44 f.
revival, 44 f.
Theravadin, 46, 67 ff., 92 f.,
    95 f., 111–115, 119, 163 ff.,
    168, 190, 201, 206
"Three Bodies" (Trikāya),
    117 ff.
Burmese, 114

Caste, 54 ff., 156 f.
Christ; *see* Jesus Christ
Christianity, 5 19, 76 81, 96–
    101, 123–128, 147–152,
    171–178
  attitudes toward other reli-
    gions, 171–178
  authority and freedom, 10 f.
  the Divine, 96–101
  divisions, 6
  "freedom of the will," 126